TOUCHY SITUATIONS

A CONVERSATION TEXT FOR ESL STUDENTS

Glen Alan Penrod

DELTA PUBLISHING COMPANY

©1993 by GLEN ALAN PENROD
Fourth Edition, ©2002

Requests for permission to make copies of any part of the work should be sent to:

DELTA PUBLISHING COMPANY
A Division of DELTA SYSTEMS CO., INC.
1400 Miller Parkway
McHenry, IL 60050 USA
(800) 323–8270 or (815) 363–3582
www.delta-systems.com

Layout and Design by Linda Bruell

Printed in the United States of America
Reprinted 2004, 2006, 2007, 2008, 2009, 2011

10 9 8 7 6

978-1-887744-74-4

To my students in Hong Kong, Hawaii, Utah, Taiwan and Korea, whose friendship and enthusiasm for learning English inspired me to write this book.

I would like to thank Vicky, Randall and Chanel for letting me set up shop in their home and office while I put this book together. I am also indebted to Janice Penner for her evaluation of the manuscript and to Timothy Sullivan, Mark Bergold, Michael Butler, Kyra Sysak, and Linda Ferderer for proofing. Finally, I would like to thank my family and friends, both in and out of the profession, whose examples, encouragement and love have sustained me through it all.

TABLE OF CONTENTS

TOUCHY SITUATIONS

INTRODUCTION

For a long time, there has been a need for advanced ESL conversation texts which provide students with both challenging linguistic material and interesting discussion topics. *Touchy Situations* is designed to fill that need. It provides conversation students with a bridge between controlled and free expression. Each lesson includes these elements:

1) preview of grammatical structures and vocabulary to be used in the context of the discussion

2) a variety of thought-provoking topics, ranging from business issues to problem-solving simulations

3) a follow-up section which enables students to extend their discussions to related topics.

With *Touchy Situations*, the teacher becomes a helpful bystander, or if he or she chooses, a participant in the activity. The teacher's main tasks are to explain the vocabulary and structures, be on hand to answer questions, provide feedback or correction, and in rare cases, to help jump-start a discussion when students can't get it going themselves.

TIPS FOR TEACHERS

Touchy Situations incorporates four main lesson formats:

> **Information Gap Activities** (Chapters 1, 5, 9, 13, 17)
> **Small Group Discussion** (Chapters 2, 6, 10, 14, 18)
> **Face-to-face Role Plays** (Chapters 3, 7, 11, 15, 19)
> **Discussion and Presentation** (Chapters 4, 8, 12, 16, 20)

In order to be most effective with the book, teachers need to understand and become comfortable with each of these formats. The lessons themselves are best suited for 90 minutes of class time. Thirty minutes is suggested for **Warm Up**, **Vocabulary Preview** and **Conversation Strategies**. Fifty to sixty minutes can be spent on the **Situation/Activity** and **Follow Up**. Since most adult ESL classes consist of either one or two hour periods, the time of the lessons can be lengthened or shortened at the discretion of the teacher. For shorter periods, **Warm Up** and **Vocabulary** sections can be assigned as preparatory homework, or parts of the lesson can be carried over to the next class meeting. For longer periods, teachers can ask students to practice the **Conversation Strategies** with a partner or write and discuss vocabulary definitions in class. For face-to-face role plays, there are more than enough situations for a full hour of discussion, so the teacher may wish to select only those situations which are most relevant or interesting to his/her students.

Rather than include lengthy teacher's notes for each chapter, I am providing sample lesson plans for the first five chapters so that teachers can become familiar with each of the lesson formats.

INTRODUCTORY LESSON: Breaking the Ice

The purpose of this chapter is to help students use their language skills to get acquainted with one another. It introduces them to phrases for starting a conversation and, more importantly, keeping it going. The focus of this chapter is not so much on the language itself as it is on helping students establish rapport with their classmates and build confidence in their speaking ability. The first lesson will set the stage for the rest of the book's activities.

The **Warm Up** and **Focus** are designed to prepare the students for the main activity. Have the students read the warm up questions and then call on a few of them to share their opinions with the class. Since many students may be unfamiliar with the lesson format, the focus will give them an idea of what to expect.

The **Conversation Strategies** provide a step-by-step approach to initiating, maintaining, and closing a conversation. The explanations and examples are brief, but you may wish to add a few contextualized examples or ask the students to provide some of their own.

For the **Activity**, it is best to arrange the chairs around the perimeter of the classroom, so that students have a large open space in the center to mingle. Have students stand up and walk around the room talking to their classmates. They must first introduce themselves, then ask additional questions to continue the conversation. Some sample questions are provided on Page 5 for students who have trouble thinking of what to say. Remind them to ask follow-up questions to keep the conversation going.

As the teacher, you may wish to control the timing of the activity so that everyone has a chance to meet each other. You can do this by saying "change partners" every few minutes. If some students do not heed the instruction, walk over, and at a natural break in their conversation, individually remind them. If there is an odd number of students, you may choose to be a participant in the activity.

After everyone has had a chance to talk with all their classmates, ask students to sit down and write what they can remember about the people they just talked to. Call on a few students to share their information with the class.

SMALL GROUP DISCUSSION: Volcanic Eruption

The purpose of this chapter is to give students a chance to practice words for common household items and introduce them to fundamental phrases for expressing opinions in small group discussions.

As a warm-up exercise, have the students look over the vocabulary list to see how many of the words they already know. An easy way to test their knowledge of the words without reverting to their first language is to have them draw pictures of the items mentioned. You may also have them write a synonym or simple definition of the new word. It is best not to spend too much class time on vocabulary because the activity requires a full fifty minute class period. The vocabulary words can be assigned as a preparatory activity.

The majority of the class time in this and every chapter should be spent on the **Situation** or **Activity** section, so you may need to go over the **Conversation Strategies** quickly or assign them as preparatory homework. The same holds true for **Vocabulary** and **Follow Up** exercises.

This is the first of five small group discussions in the book. Since this chapter will set the foundation for future discussions of this type, it is important that students learn the strategies for expressing and supporting opinions well. Groups should be small enough (3 to 4 students) that everyone gets a chance to talk. Once you have divided the class up into small groups, you are free to move around among groups and listen to students talking, explain vocabulary words, or offer correction where necessary. You may also want to monitor the groups to make sure that everyone has an equal opportunity to speak.

FACE-TO-FACE ROLE PLAY: Best Friends

This chapter gives students practice with extended one-on-one conversations. To begin with, ask the class the **Warm Up** questions on the first page of the chapter. Then go over the **Vocabulary** words, modeling pronunciation and having students repeat. As with other lessons, you may assign students to define unfamiliar words in preparation for the class activity. The activity itself will probably take a full hour. I have purposely provided many role play situations so that you can choose the ones most suitable for your students.

Go over the **Conversation Strategies**, explaining that these will be used in the activity. Answer any questions the students might have. For this type of activity, it is best to arrange the chairs in two long rows facing each other. Explain that the people sitting in one row will be **B** and those in the other row will be **A**. **B** is the person with a problem; **A** is the best friend, who will help his/her partner solve the problem. As they proceed with the activity, students may switch roles for each new situation. It is best to give them a set amount of time (4 minutes is suggested) for each separate role play. It is also important that the timing is consistent and that students do not go ahead to the next role play until you tell them to do so. After they have done three or four role plays with the same partners, have them switch to a new "best friend." This can be done easily by having the A's move one seat to the right or the B's move one seat to the left.

DISCUSSION AND PRESENTATION: Financing the Twins

The purpose of this chapter is to give students practice in organizing and presenting their ideas. The lesson takes the small group discussion a step further and has the students prepare to share their conclusions with the class. As in most chapters in the book, there are **Warm Up** questions and **Vocabulary** words to help focus the students' attention.

Review the **Conversation Strategies** from Chapter 2 and introduce the new ones for this chapter. Page 23 gives some strategies for controlling a discussion and suggests that you appoint group leaders. The group leaders can make sure that all points get discussed in the allotted time, but aren't absolutely necessary. It is more important that all students know how to lead a discussion. Divide students into small groups (three or four) and have them read over the situation and discuss the options in preparation for making their presentation.

The last page of the chapter gives strategies for organizing a short presentation and a sample outline. Tell the students that someone in each group will deliver a short (one minute) presentation of his/her group's conclusion to the class. To ensure that each student prepares, do not assign students beforehand. Call on them when it is time for their group's presentation.

INFORMATION GAP: What's My Crime?

This chapter will give students practice asking and responding to yes/no questions in creative ways. It will also let them exercise their skills with different word forms.

The chapter consists of an **Information Gap** activity which requires a little advanced preparation by both teacher and students. Before the class begins, you will need to prepare 18 small cards or slips of paper; each with the name of a different crime from the Activity page of the chapter. These cards will be distributed to students to let them know what their secret crimes are. Since the **Vocabulary** words for this chapter are quite difficult, I recommend assigning students to look them up before class. Then, you can quickly review the list for pronunciation and clarification. Also, explain or write on the board the **Conversation Strategies** for asking and answering yes/no questions.

For the activity, students play the roles of both criminal and detective. Their task is to find out what crimes the other students committed while trying to conceal their own. They do this by circulating around the room and asking each other yes/no questions. When they discover a classmate's crime, they should write his/her name down in the blank next to the crime.

Follow Up activities for this chapter include a Word Form exercise and additional questions for further discussion.

II. CONVERSATION STRATEGIES

INTRODUCTIONS

Before you can start asking a lot of questions of someone you don't know, it is polite to introduce yourself. A sample introduction is presented below.

> A: I don't believe we've met. I'm _____
> B: And I'm _____. Nice to meet you.
> A: Good to meet you too.

OPENING LINES

To get a conversation started, you may ask questions regarding the situation that brings you together, or you may ask general questions about the other person's background. For example:

> **Have you studied here before?**
> **What brings you to** Philadelphia?
> **How do you know** Sally (the hostess)?
> **Is this your first** TESOL Convention?
> **What do you do for a living?**
> **How do you like** Massachusetts?

KEEPING THE CONVERSATION GOING

Good conversation skills require that you listen as well as speak. Listening indicates that you have genuine interest in what your partner has to say. Some common phrases which are used to show interest are

> **Oh really?**
> **That's interesting.**
> **Is that right?**

Another way to show interest and encourage your partner to talk is to ask for details. To ask for more details, use information questions:

Why . . . ?	Who . . . ?
How . . . ?	What . . . ?
When . . . ?	How long . . . ?
Where . . . ?	How often . . . ?

CHAPTER 1

BREAKING THE ICE

I. WARM UP

Which of these topics are appropriate to discuss when you meet someone for the first time? Which ones are inappropriate?

	APPROPRIATE	INAPPROPRIATE
A person's age		✓
Marital status		✓
Occupation	✓	
Salary		✓
College major	✓	
Weight		✓
Family	✓	
Hobbies and pastimes	✓	
Political opinions		✓
Common interests	✓	

FOCUS

For you to get the most out of this book, it is important that you establish a good communicative relationship with your classmates and teacher. This introductory chapter is designed to help you get acquainted with your classmates while you exercise your English skills. The questions *(adj) brought into social contact* in the activity will help you get a conversation started. However, it is up to you to keep the conversation going once it has begun. As you walk around the room and mingle with your classmates, do *(v) socialized, chit chat* not limit yourself to the questions in the book; ask follow-up questions to show that you are interested in what the other person has to say. If you feel a little shy about speaking English at first, don't worry. Your classmates probably feel the same way. Challenge yourself to speak more; you'll make some new friends in the process.

For example, if your partner expresses an interest in fishing, you might ask him/her to elaborate by asking:

> Where do you usually go fishing?
> **How often** do you go?
> **When** is the best time to go?
> **Who** do you like to go with?

If you have been talking for a long time, it is polite to ask the other person about himself/herself. This can be done in many ways. A few sample phrases are given below.

> How about you, Jack? What do you like to do on weekends?
> How about yourself? Do you like skiing too?
> Yourself? Have you ever been abroad?
> What about you, Jill? Are you a surfer too?

REMEMBERING NAMES

If you have forgotten someone's name, ask him/her again. You might say:

> What did you say your name was?
> How do you spell it?
> I'm sorry, I forgot your name.
> What was your name again?

CLOSING A CONVERSATION

Since in this activity you are required to talk to as many of your classmates as possible, it is important for you to know how to close a conversation. Some polite phrases for closing a conversation are:

> It's been good talking to you.
> Nice talking to you, Janet.
> Glad to make your acquaintance, Mr. Simpson.

NOTE: If you repeat the person's name when closing a conversation, you will remember it better. Also, it will show that you are happy to have met him/her.

III. THE ACTIVITY

Walk around the room and get acquainted with your classmates. Introduce yourself first, then ask a few opening questions. If you have trouble thinking of topics, you may use some of the ones listed below. Remember, these questions are only to help you get a conversation started. It is your responsibility to keep the conversation going. Your teacher will tell you when to change partners.

1. Where are you from?

2. How long have you been in (this area)?

3. How do you like it here?

4. How did you find out about this class?

5. Have you taken classes here before?

6. What type of work do you do?

7. What do you like to study?

8. Do you have any unusual hobbies?

9. Have you read any interesting books lately?

10. Do you know . . . (name of a person with similar background as your partner)?

11. Tell me about your family.

12. Where do you usually go after work/class?

14. What do you like to do in your free time?

15. What did you do on your last vacation/day off?

16. What is something you have never done but would like to do?

17. What is something you have done but never want to do again?

18. What would you be doing if you weren't in class right now?

IV. WINDING DOWN

When you have finished talking with everyone, write down some interesting things you have learned about your classmates. Try to remember as much as you can. Your teacher may call on you to share your information with the class.

Sample Sentences:

Mary is a beautician at Harris Dunn Beauty Salon .
Barry has never been scuba diving, but he would like to try it sometime.
Mr. Perry lives in the suburbs and travels 40 minutes to work every day.
Teri would like to meet the President.

What did you find out about your classmates?

1. _____

_____

2. _____

_____

3. _____

_____

4. _____

_____

5. _____

_____

6. _____

_____

7. _____

_____

8. _____

_____

9. _____

_____

10. _____

_____

CHAPTER 2

VOLCANIC ERUPTION

I. WARM UP

The following words will appear in this chapter. Draw a picture, give a synonym or write a short definition beside the words you know.

volcano	carpenter
erupt (v) to burst forth, to eject matter	breadwinner (n) a person supporting his or her family with the money he/she makes
resident (n) a person who resides in a place.	document
radius (n) a straight line extending from the center of a circle or sphere to the circum or surface	deceased (n) the particular dead person or persons refer to (adj) no longer living; dead
threaten (v) to be a source of danger to someone or sth.	razor
destruction (n) the act of destroying, the condition of being destroyed	tropical
evacuation (n) the act or process of discharge, the removal of persons or things from an endangered area	jewelry
shelter	irreplaceable (adj) incapable of being replaced; unique
chopper (helicopter) informal word of helicopter	aquarium
minivan	bulk (n), the greater part, main mass or body, thickness
autograph (n) a painting, drawing, sculpture or photograph portrait of someone, especially of the face	dimension
autograph	vehicle
(adj) weakly emotional, expressive of or sentimental appealing to sentiment especially the tender emotions and feelings	microwave oven
utensil	record album
rifle	portable
ammunition (n) anything such as bullets, rockets, bombs, missiles chemicals that can be fired from a weapon.	entertainment

II. CONVERSATION STRATEGIES

OPINIONS AND SUPPORT

There are many ways to express your ideas and give support for them. The easiest is to state your opinion. Then follow it directly with a supporting statement.

OPINION	REASON/SUPPORT
I think we should take the bedding.	We could get cold at night.
I don't think we need to take the dog.	He can run along behind the car.

Always be prepared to back up your statements with supporting details. If a member of your group fails to give support for his opinion, gently remind him/her by asking "Why?" or "Why do you think… / Why don't you think…"

Example: A: I think we should take the carpentry tools.
             B: Why do you think we need to take them?
             A: Because we can use them to build a new house.

MAKING SUGGESTIONS

MILD SUGGESTIONS

Why **don't we** take the first aid kit?

Why **not** take the cooking utensils?

How about ⎯ ⎯ ⎯ ⎯ ⎯ ⎯

(The above statements appear negative, but they are positive suggestions.)

Isn't it better ⎯ ⎯ ⎯ ⎯

Let's take the camping equipment.

Let's not take the children's toys.

I recommend

It would be a good idea to take the aquarium.

Don't you think we should take the bottled water?

Don't you think it would be a good idea to take a camera?

STRONGER SUGGESTIONS   sth that you sure about it

We'd better take the kitchen sink.

We'd better not forget the children's clothing.

I prefer

I highly recommend

we should

VERY STRONG SUGGESTIONS

We've **got to** take the microwave oven.

We are **NOT** leaving the piano behind!

We **definitely** need to take the stamp collection.

We have to

we must

EXPRESSING DIFFERENT POINTS OF VIEW

Not everyone thinks alike. A discussion would not be very interesting if they did. If you have a different opinion than a classmate's, it is all right to express it. You may simply say, "I agree/I disagree," then state the reason. Make sure that your facial expression and tone of voice convey a positive attitude toward the person you're speaking to.

DIRECT DISAGREEMENT

Short or abrupt statements often convey rudeness or stubbornness in English:

That's a dumb idea.

That's not right.

It is best not to use these types of expressions in friendly discussions. A better way to express a differing point of view is to use longer statements and give your reasons.

For example:

A: **I don't think that's such a good idea.**

B: Why not?

A: Because someone might get hurt.

Another way is to use questions:

A: **Don't you think it would be better if** we took the dining
room set and left the lawyer's books? After all, we need to eat.

B: You have a good point there.

A: **Are you sure** you want to take the house plants?

B: Of course. We can't leave them here to die.

Disagree

Polite	Impolite
In my opinion. — .	that's a dumb idea
I think it's better — .	That's not right
I would like . . . —	
I prefer. — . —	
What do you think if . . . —	
I don't think that's such a good idea because — —	
Don't you think it would be better _ _ _ _ _	

FOCUS

In the next few pages, you will be given a situation to discuss with a small group. Use as many of the Conversation Strategies as you can but don't feel limited to only them.

Be creative and try some of your own expressions. Your teacher will come around to offer correction and help when necessary.

Read through the situation as a class. Then be prepared to discuss it in your small groups. You may want to repeat the bold-faced vocabulary words for pronunciation.

III. THE SITUATION

Mount Blastoff is **threatening** to **erupt**. Scientists estimate that it could blow anytime within the next twenty-four hours. You and your family live within five miles of the volcano. As you sit down to dinner, you hear the following announcement over the radio:

<u>Residents</u> of the Mount Blastoff area:

The volcano could erupt in the next four hours. Everything within
a ten mile **radius** is in danger of partial or complete **destruction**. We
(n) the act of destroying
ask that everyone leave the area immediately. In order to insure a
discharge
speedy and orderly **evacuation**, we ask that residents of this area
take Highway 911 north to the government **shelter** at Safe Haven.
helicopter
Choppers will be on hand to transport those without their own **vehicles**.
discharge
We repeat: <u>EVACUATE</u> THE AREA IMMEDIATELY!

*the removal of persons or things
from an endanger area*

IV. YOUR OBJECTIVE

(adj) involving an extremely important decision or result

Your family must make some **crucial** decisions in a very short time. Luckily, you have a large **minivan** which can hold many of your **belongings**. You estimate that you can have it loaded and ready to go in about 30 minutes. Obviously, you cannot take everything with you. You must decide which of the following items you will take and which you will leave behind. The van will hold only 3,000 pounds before it breaks down, and some **bulky** items will take up too much space. Don't overload the vehicle. *(See note on page 11.)* Good luck. The clock is ticking away...

ITEMS TO CHOOSE FROM			
ITEM	WEIGHT	BULK	VALUE
1. Husband, 45 years old	220 lbs.	****	excellent cook, part-time carpenter
2. Wife, 39 years old	130	***	breadwinner, lawyer
3. Susan, 9 years old	60	**	
4. Billy, 4 years old	35	*	
5. Guffy (family dog)	50	**	
6. Large portrait of deceased grandparent	5	**	sentimental value
7. Metal box containing family documents	15	**	irreplaceable
8. Six month supply of food	350	******	
9. Children's clothing	150	****	
10. Parents' clothing	300	*****	
11. Stamp collection	140	***	over $7500
12. Autographed Elvis Presley record album	1	*	$250 (at present)
13. Children's toys	100	***	
14. Lawyer's books	600	****	
15. Bottled water	25	***	
16. Gardening tools	15	***	
17. Television	10	**	
18. Large Oriental vase	25	***	
19. Refrigerator	450	******	
20. Carpentry tools	50	***	

ITEMS TO CHOOSE FROM (cont.)				
	ITEM	WEIGHT	BULK	VALUE
21.	Piano	800	********	family heirloom
22.	Guitar	10	**	
23.	Cooking utensils	10	**	
24.	Dishes	50	***	
25.	Wife's jewelry box	5	*	$1,000 (mostly fake diamonds)
26.	Microwave oven	20	**	
27.	Family first aid kit	5	*	
28.	Rifle and ammunition	10	**	
29.	Bedding (sheets, pillows, blankets)	50	***	
30.	Bathroom supplies	20	**	
31.	Bicycle (girls', 24 inch tires)	50	****	
32.	Tropical fish tank (aquarium)	50	***	
33.	Folding table and chairs (dining room set)	100	***	
34.	Exercise equipment	700	*****	
35.	Portable stove and fuel	35	**	
36.	Computer and printer	20	***	
37.	Camping equipment	80	***	
38.	House plants	50	**	
39.	Sofa (couch)	200	******	
40.	Kitchen sink	80	***	

NOTE: The minivan can hold up to 3000 pounds, but not many bulky items. It will not hold more than 45 stars (*). (Stars indicate the relative size of objects. Items with large dimensions are identified by more stars in the "Bulk" column.)

V. FOLLOW UP

At the end of the discussion, make a list of the items you chose. Be prepared to tell the class why you chose the items that you did and why you didn't choose the others.

ITEM   REASON FOR SELECTION

1. _____
   _____

2. _____
   _____

3. _____
   _____

4. _____
   _____

5. _____
   _____

6. _____
   _____

7. _____
   _____

8. _____
   _____

9. _____
   _____

10. _____
    _____

11. _____
    _____

12. _____
    _____

13. _____

    _____

14. _____

    _____

15. _____

    _____

CHAPTER 3

BEST FRIENDS

H.W.

I. WARM UP

Discuss the following questions as a class:

If you had a serious problem, whom would you go to for help? *my husband*

Would you be willing to discuss anything with that person? *Yes, I feel confortable to discuss with him*

What if he/she were the problem? Could you talk to him/her openly about it? *Yes, I would openly talk with him*

How honest are you when discussing unpleasant subjects? *I am very honest with my feeling to open the problem with him*

FOCUS

In this chapter, you will practice conversation strategies for openly and tactfully discussing difficult situations. You will also learn techniques for showing surprise and giving advice.

H.W.

II. VOCABULARY PREVIEW/PRONUNCIATION

The following words will appear in this chapter. Pronounce them after your teacher and define the ones you know. Compare your definitions with those of your classmates. Your teacher may ask you to consult the dictionary or a native speaker of English for definitions of any unfamiliar words.

spouse *partner*	merchandise *Product*	insomnia *cannot sleep*
confront *(v) to stand or come in front of, to face in hostility or defiance*	snorkeling	vice versa *(adv) or so หรือ conversely, contrariwise the other way around*
gambling	upset	tactfully *having or manifesting tact*
best man	maid of honor	scratch *mark*
collision *(n) a clash, a coming violently into contact*	amazing	incredible *amazing*
ridiculous	disgusting	co-worker
picky	bad breath	geometry *the branch of mathematic*

↑ a keen sense of what to say or do to avoid giving offense

Ex vice versa
children should respect theirs parents and vice versa

คือ ถ้า homo[...]สัมพันธ์เหมือน

that deals with deduction of the properties, measurement, and relationship of point, lines, angles, and figures in space from their defining condition by means of certain assumed

III. CONVERSATION STRATEGIES

CONVERSATION STARTERS

There are several phrases in English which are used to start a conversation. A few of them are listed below.

What's new? (Used when you haven't seen someone for a while. It means "has anything interesting happened since I last saw you?")

A: Guess what? (This means "I have something interesting to tell you.")
B: What? ("Go ahead. Tell me.")

Examples:

A: What's new?
B: Not much. How about you?
A: I just got a new job.
B: Congratulations! That's great...

A: Guess what?
B: What?
A: I lost my wallet yesterday.
B: Oh. That's too bad....

Practice:

With a partner, practice these situations using "Guess what?" or "What's new?"

<u>Situation 1</u>
You got an A on your geometry test. Tell your partner the good news.

<u>Situation 2</u>
You won a gold medal at the Winter Olympics. Tell your partner about it.

<u>Situation 3</u>
Your brother broke his leg while playing hockey last week. Tell your partner the news.

REJOINDERS

Rejoinders are used when responding to what someone has just told you. Some of the most common rejoinders in English are:

Really? That's great! / That's wonderful. (for good news)
That's too bad. / I'm sorry to hear that. (for bad news)

Other rejoinders are formed by repeating the subject pronoun along with the first auxiliary verb of the corresponding question. See the examples below.

You are?
You did?
She is?

They don't?
He isn't?
You haven't?

properties of space

Pronoun first auxiliary

A: Jeremy is in the hospital.
B: He is?

A: The Adamsons will move to Delaware.
B: They will?

A: Janice lives in Vancouver.
B: She does?

A: I left my wallet on the bus.
B: You did?

A: Jay isn't coming to the meeting.
B: He isn't?

A: I don't ride a motorcycle anymore.
B: You don't?

Practice making statements and rejoinders with a partner.

It is important to add a follow-up question after the rejoinder. For example:

A: I just got back from Florida.
B: You did? **How was it?**
A: Wonderful. We went snorkeling for three days in a row.

A: My husband got a new job.
B: He did? **What kind of** job did he get?

USING DETAILS

Include details to make the conversation more interesting. Use your imagination to fill in the specifics of a story.

= uninteresting

Dull: Yesterday I had an accident.

More interesting: Last night while I was driving home, I was hit by a drunk driver going 80 miles an hour on the freeway. Luckily, I was wearing a seat belt.

✵ SHOWING SURPRISE

Rejoinders with heavy rising intonation indicate surprise. For example:

a clash

A: My daughter was involved in a three-car collision.
B: She WAS? Is she all right?
A: A few minor scratches, but other than that, she's okay.

Sometimes Wh- question words following the pronoun and verb indicate added surprise. For example:

He did WHAT?   They went WHERE?

Other phrases for showing surprise are:

> You're kidding!
> I can't believe it.
> That's amazing/incredible/ really something.

Similar phrases can be used to show <u>contempt</u>. *→ the stated that show the loss respect, honor*

> That's ridiculous/crazy/disgusting.

Example:

> A: Guess what? *conversation starter*
> B: What?
> A: I was fired from work today.
> B: You were? What happened? *→ follow up question after rejoinder* *using details*   *rejoinder →*
> A: I forgot to lock the doors last <u>night and</u> someone walked away with $50,000 in cash.
> B: You're kidding! *→ showing surprise*
> A: No, I'm serious. The boss told me not to come to the office anymore.
> B: That sounds terrible. Why don't you...

✳ POLITE APPROACHES ✳

If you want to talk, but the other person seems busy, it is polite to ask if he/she has time. Use phrases like these:

> → Can I talk to you for a minute?
> → Do you have a minute?
> → Do you mind if I ask you a few questions?
> → *I'm sorry to bother you, but - - - -*

Example:

> A: Do you have a minute?
> B: Sure. What's on your mind?
> A: Well, it's about my wife....

BRINGING UP THE SUBJECT

It is <u>often difficult to bring up an unpleasant subject</u>. Some useful phrases for this are listed below.

> There's something I think you should know.
> I don't know how to tell you this, but...
> I hate to tell you this, but...
> *It's hard to say this*

Jตมมาๆ 52)

Sometimes a more direct approach is <u>appropriate</u>:

Mark, I have a problem.

Remember that gold watch I borrowed from you last week?

ASKING FOR ADVICE

The following are common ways of asking a close friend for advice:

What would you do, If you were me

What do you think I should do?

What should I do about...?

What would *you* do (in this situation)?

What is your opinion

GIVING ADVICE

Some of the most common phrases for giving advice are:

Maybe you should...

I think you should...

If I were you, I'd...

It might be a good idea to...

Why don't you...

Examples:

A: **Guess what?** → *Conversation Starter*

B: What?

A: I'm going to get married next week!

B: You are? → *rejoinders*

A: Yes. Bob and I just met, and we're madly in love!

B: Have you told your parents yet?   → *asking for advice*

A: Yes, but they say I'm too young. **What do you think I should do?**

B: Well, **I think you should...** → *giving advice*

C: I'm having trouble with Cristy. She sleeps in until 8:30 every morning. Then she is in a bad mood when I try to get her ready for school.

giving advice

D: **Maybe you should** get her an alarm clock.

C: Good idea. Why didn't I think of that?

IV. YOUR OBJECTIVE

①your friend give you an advice

You and your partner are best friends. Either you or your friend has a problem. Act out (role play)
(by myself)
the following situations in which you give your friend advice or vice versa. You have approximately
four minutes for each situation. Your teacher will tell you when to change to a new partner.

V. THE SITUATIONS

*A: Guess what?
B: What?*

1. Your friend would like to be movie star, but you don't think he/she has enough talent.
Advise him/her to choose another profession. (Start: "Guess what? ...?")

*A: I would like to be movie star. B: You would? Are you sure? A: Yes B: I think you need more
experience enough
How about you try - - - -*

2. You borrowed your best friend's gold watch (worth $3,500) last week and lost it.
You have looked everywhere, but cannot find it. What do you tell him/her?
(Begin: "I don't know how to tell you this, but... ")

_____

3. Your best friend's **spouse** called and asked you to talk to your friend about his/her
gambling problem. Discuss the problem with your friend. (Begin: "Can I talk to you for
a minute?...")

_____

4. Your friend has **bad breath**. He/She is having a hard time getting any dates and
comes to you for advice. What do you tell him/her?

_____

5. You left some important notes for your exam on your desk at school. The school
building is now locked and your test is tomorrow. Ask your friend what to do.

_____

6. Your spouse is paying too much attention to his/her **co-workers** of the opposite sex.
Ask your friend what you should do.

_____

7. Your friend's spouse does not like the two of you talking so much on the telephone.
Discuss the situation with your friend.

_____

8. Your friend borrowed your **power saw** five months ago and still hasn't returned it.
Confront him/her about it.

_____

9. You are going to get married but will ask someone else (not your best friend) to be
your **best man/maid of honor**. Tell him/her the news.

_____

10. Your friend accidentally took some **merchandise** worth $25.00 from a drug store and
forgot to pay for it. He/She asks you what to do.

11. You want to move in with your boyfriend/girlfriend but know your parents will be **upset** if you do. Ask your best friend for advice.

_____

12. Your friend has **insomnia** and consequently is always late for work. You worry that he/she might lose his/her job. Talk to him/her about it.

_____

13. Your friend's ex–husband/wife is interested in dating you, but you don't want a relationship with him/her. Ask your friend what to do.

_____

14. You accidently ran over your spouse's favorite pet with your jeep. Ask your friend what you should do.

VI. EXTENSION

Think of your own "touchy situations" and role play them with a partner.

CHAPTER 4

FINANCING THE TWINS

I. WARM UP

Indicate whether you **agree** or **disagree** with these statements.

_A___ 1. The best person to take care of a child is its own mother.

_A___ 2. Fathers should divide child care equally with mothers.

_A___ 3. Females are better **baby sitters** than males are.

_D___ 4. A career woman should quit her job when she has a baby.

_D___ 5. Grandparents should play a major role in the care of their grandchildren.

_D___ 6. It is okay to let someone outside the family be a child's primary caretaker.

_A___ 7. Men are just as good at child care as women are.

_A___ 8. One parent should be granted parental leave from his/her job after a baby is born.

FOCUS

This chapter will let you explore the **dilemma** of family finances and child care responsibilities while introducing you to some common strategies for discussion and presentation.

II. VOCABULARY PREVIEW/PRONUNCIATION

a situation requiring a choice between equally undesirable alternatives / any difficult or perplexing situation or problem

baby sitter	(n) dilemma	pregnant
overexertion =	suspicion	maternity leave *Time off work to have and take care of a baby*
financial	heartbeat	clinic
liquor	nutritious	get along
split	series	checkup
(n) a list, plan; things to be done agenda	income	nanny
adopt	participate	implement

to put forth or into use as power; exercise

If A, then D; if C then D. Either A or C. Therefore either B or D"

(v) fulfilment, to put into action

EX The new law will be implemented at the schools.

III. CONVERSATION STRATEGIES

This chapter gives you a chance to discuss your opinion in groups. Some phrases to introduce an opinion are:

In my opinion…

I believe that/I don't believe that…

It seems to me that…

I prefer

I recommed

It's better / I think it's better I suggest

As a matter of fact

How about

✱ ⟶

DISCUSSING OPTIONS

When you have a given set of options, you may refer to them directly:

One of the best things about Option 7 is…

Plan A is good/important because…

This option allows…

you can achieve the best result if

This option allows

AGREEING

One way to express agreement is to acknowledge the idea, then repeat or paraphrase it. For example:

I agree / Absolutely / sounds good

You're alright

You have a good point there. The father can't afford to quit his job.

I think Timothy's right. It isn't a good idea to split up the family.

That's The best choice

You may wish to add a follow-up question. For example:

Good point. Where do we go from there?

Not a bad idea. How will we implement it?

RAISING CONCERNS

If you want to bring up a concern about a particular point, you may use phrases such as:

The problem with that is money. Who will finance it?

That raises the problem/issue of hiring outside help. How are we going to deal with that?

On the other hand, it might not solve the real problem.

What do you think if ____

How about ____ / What about ____

first of all ____

What if

Questions are another good way to raise concerns:

> **What about** cost?
>
> **What are we going to do about** cost?
>
> **Have you considered** what it will cost?
>
> **Do you realize** how much that would cost?
>
> **Do you really think** that's such a good idea?

What are the pros and cons ?
(good) (bad)

ASKING FOR INPUT

It is important that each member of the group has a chance to express his/her opinion. If some members are not **participating**, you may encourage them with phrases like:

What do you suggest ?   *Would you like to say sth.*

> **How about you** Simon, do you agree with that?
>
> **What do the rest of you think?**
>
> **Do you have any thoughts on that,** Esther?

What's your opinion ?
What do you think ?

CONTROLLING THE DISCUSSION

When you have an **agenda** or a set amount of time for discussion, it is important that you use your time wisely. Otherwise, you may not get around to all the main points.

Some discussions are controlled by a group leader or person in charge. For this exercise, your teacher may appoint one member as group leader. The group leader can manipulate the course of the discussion by using such phrases as

> **We'll start by** looking at Option 1
>
> **Let's look at** Plan C.
>
> **Let's move on** to Proposal 4

everyone on the same page

SEEKING CONSENSUS

A good discussion leader will sometimes seek **consensus** before moving on to the next point. Some phrases for doing this are

> Should we move on to Option 5?
>
> Okay, are you all ready for the next option?
>
> Any more ideas on Plan D?

Do we all agree ____

Is everybody okay with ___ ?

= to make extra time for sth

STALLING THE DISCUSSION

If you have an objection to moving on , you may say something like:

> **Before we move on,** I think we should look again at…
>
> **Wait a minute.** We still need to consider…

CONCLUDING

In conversation, the words so and then can have a concluding effect when followed by a short pause.

For this effect, use so at the beginning of a statement and then at the end of a phrase. For example:

> **So…,** the best option is number 8.
>
> **So…,** we all agree on Proposal E.
>
> **All right then,** let's wrap it up.
>
> **Let's bring it to a close then.**
>
> **In summary then,…**

OK, Let do it

We agree that this is a best option

IV. THE SITUATION

Read over the following situation and be prepared to discuss it with your group.

H.W.
Read for
Mon Sep 11 2016

Mr. and Mrs. Tandem are overjoyed. After years of waiting for a child, Mrs. Tandem is at last **pregnant.** She has been taking good care of her health, avoiding **liquor** and **overexertion** and making sure she has a **nutritious** and balanced diet. Just last week when Mrs. Tandem went to the **clinic** for her checkup, Dr. Goodnews told her that he **detected** not one, but two tiny **heartbeats** inside. After a **series** of tests, he confirmed his **suspicion.** Mrs. Tandem is going to have twins. She and her husband are very excited, but they face a **dilemma.** They have prepared well for one child, but how can they handle two? Mr. Tandem was planning on quitting his job as a school teacher to take care of the new baby, but with the added expenses, he doesn't think that would be such a good idea. Mrs. Tandem cantake two months of **maternity leave** when the children are born, but she cannot leave her job as a corporate executive without causing serious **financial** problems for the family. What do you think the Tandems should do?

to discover in the performance of some act

(n) act of suspecting

V. YOUR OBJECTIVE

Discuss the options below with the members of your group. It is best to first outline the **pros** and **cons** of the option and talk about each one before moving on to the next option. After discussing all the options thoroughly, try to reach a group consensus on which option is best and be prepared to present the reasons for your choice to the rest of the class.

OPTION 1

Mr. Tandem quits his job and becomes a full-time house husband.

Pro: - Someone will be with the kids 24 hours a day.
- No one outside the family will need to be involved.

Con: - Loss of **income** when Mr. Tandem quits his job.
- Mr. Tandem cannot breast-feed the infants.

OPTION 2

Send the twins to Mr. Tandem's parents' home (sixty miles away) for the week and bring them home on the weekends.

Pro:

Con:

OPTION 3

Borrow money from Mrs. Tandem's rich uncle.

Pro:

Con:

✳ OPTION 4

Hire a live-in **nanny**.

Pro:

Con:

OPTION 5

Ask Mr. Tandem's mother to come and stay with the family during the week.
(Mrs. Tandem and her mother-in-law do not **get along** well.)

Pro:

Con:

OPTION 6

Allow Mrs. Tandem's childless sister to **adopt** one of the twins.

Pro:

Con:

✳ ## OPTION 7

Move into a smaller, cheaper home.

Pro:

Con:

✳ OTHER OPTIONS Mr. Tandem quit his job and become to do ^ebay online business at home with a full time house husband

Pro:

Con:

VI. PRESENTATION STRATEGIES

After you have discussed each option in your small groups, you will be asked to present your findings to the rest of the class. Your teacher will probably call on one person to represent the group, but it is important that everyone be prepared. Presentation is not as difficult as you might think. First, make a statement which indicates the decision of your group, then give reasons to support your statement. Structure your presentation with transition words and phrases:

SAMPLE PRESENTATION OUTLINE

GENERAL STATEMENT ①
Our group has decided that the best alternative is Option 1

SUPPORTING IDEAS ②
This option is best for several reasons:

> **First, First of all, In the first place, One reason is...**
> Someone would be with the twins full-time.
> This is important because...

> **Second, Next, Another reason is...**
> The Tandems could save a lot of money on child care.
> They wouldn't have to hire anyone.

> **Third, Then, Also**
> Children need to bond with their own parents.

3 reason on pros

CONTRASTING IDEAS ②③

> **On the other hand, However,**
> There are some disadvantages to Option 1.
> Mr. Tandem will have to give up his job.

> **Even though/although**
> **Even though** their income will be reduced, they can still cover their expenses.
> She can keep her job **although** she may have to cut her working hours.

3 reason on cons

NOTE: Some students say *Even though..., but....* This is INCORRECT in English. Do not use *even though/although* and *but* together in the same sentence.)

CONCLUDING ⑧

> **Therefore, Thus,**
> (We concluded) that Option 1 is the best choice.

CHAPTER 5

WHAT'S MY CRIME?

I. WARM UP

Find out the meanings of the following words by looking them up in the dictionary or by asking a native speaker of English to help you define them.

theft *(n) the act of stealing; the wrongful taking and carrying away of the personal goods or property of another; larceny*	counterfeit
robbery *(n) the act, the practice, or an instance of robbing*	forgery
burglary *(n) the felony of breaking into and entering the house of another at night with intent to steal; extended by statute to cover the breaking into and entering of any of various building, by night or day*	espionage
pickpocket *(n) a person who steals money, wallets, etc. from the pocket of people as in crowded public places*	assailant
kidnap *(v) to steal, carry off, or abduct by force or fraud, especially for use as a hostage or to extract ransom*	violence
rape	enforce
murder	penalty
assault	victim
shoplifting	compensate
embezzlement	reputation
vandalism	stingy
extortion	conceal
slander	detective
smuggling	weapon
arson	fist

II. CONVERSATION STRATEGIES

In this activity, you will need to ask and respond to yes/no questions in order to find out useful and relevant information. Some sample yes/no questions are listed below.

Did your crime involve money?

      violence?

Did you do something which hurt Mr. Rich's business?

      family?

      Mr. Rich himself?

Did you damage Mr. Rich's property?

      reputation?

Did you steal anything?

Was your crime committed in broad daylight?

      after dark?

Was it committed indoors?

      outdoors?

| CREATIVE ANSWERS TO YES/NO QUESTIONS ||
AFFIRMATIVE	NEGATIVE
Uh-húh (nod your head)	Úh-uh (shake your head)
Mmh-hmmh (stress second syllable)	Mmh-mmh (stress first syllable)
Yeah. (informal)	Nope. (informal)
It sure did. (emphatic)	Of course not.
It sure was.	Absolutely not. (very emphatic)

ASKING FOR ADDITIONAL HELP	
Can you give me a hint?	Give me a clue.

NOTE: *commit a crime:* do something seriously against the law

      criminal: a person who commits a crime

EXPRESSING OTHER POSSIBILITIES

In some cases, the answer to a question may not be a clear-cut yes or no, or it may depend on individual circumstances. In such instances, you can say something like:

I didn't commit my crime at night, but I *could* have.

It wasn't done indoors, but it *might* have been.

You could say so. (closer to "yes")

Not necessarily. (closer to "no")

CONFIRMING A GUESS

When a person has made a correct guess, you can use phrases such as these to confirm:

You'(ve) got it!

(That's) right.

(Yup,) that's it.

III. THE SITUATION

Mr. Rich is the wealthiest man in town. He is also very **stingy**. Everyone in the community hates him. During the past year, a series of crimes have been committed against him and his family. Those crimes are listed on the following page.

IV. YOUR OBJECTIVE

In this activity you will be both a criminal and a **detective**. You must find out who did what to Mr. Rich, his company and his family. Your teacher will give you a card or piece of paper indicating what your secret crime was. Everyone in the class will have a different crime.

The object is to determine what crimes the others committed while trying to conceal your own. As a detective in this activity, you can ask your classmates only yes/no questions to find out what their crimes are. As a criminal, you must answer questions truthfully, but you don't have to give away any information that is not requested.

PROCEDURE

Walk around the classroom **interrogating** each of your classmates to find out what their crimes were. Remember, you may ask only yes/no questions and do not have to supply any information that is not asked for. Also, do not ask "Are you a (thief, arsonist, etc.)?" unless you have asked several preliminary questions and are reasonably sure that the answer will be "yes."

V. ACTIVITY

Can you figure out who committed these crimes? Write your classmates' names in the blanks when you discover what their crimes were.

1. _____ is a **kidnapper**. He/She kidnapped Mr. Rich's son.

2. _____ is a **burglar**. He/She burglarized Mr. Rich's house.

3. _____ is an **arsonist**. He/She burned down Mr. Rich's factory.

4. _____ is a **thief**. He/She stole Mrs. Rich's jewelry.

5. _____ is a **vandal**. He/She vandalized Mr. Rich's car.

6. _____ is a **pickpocket**. He/She stole Mr. Rich's wallet.

7. _____ is a **robber**. He/She robbed one of Mr. Rich's banks.

8. _____ is an **assailant**. He/She assaulted Mr. Rich with a weapon.

9. _____ is an **assailant**. He/She punched Mr. Rich with his/her fist.

10. _____ is a **slanderer**. He/She told lies about Mr. Rich in public.

11. _____ is an **embezzler**. He/She embezzled $20 million from Mr. Rich's company.

12. _____ is a **shoplifter**. He/She stole a lot of merchandise from one of Mr. Rich's department stores.

13. _____ is a **drug dealer**. He/She sold drugs to Mr. Rich's daughter

14. _____ is a **counterfeiter**. He/She printed money and exchanged it for Mr. Rich's real money.

15. _____ is a **forger**. He/She forged Mr. Rich's signature on checks worth $10,000.

16. _____ is a **smuggler**. He/She smuggled Mr. Rich's goods out of the country.

17. _____ is an **extortionist**. He/She forced Mr. Rich to pay him/her $50 million.

18. _____ is a **murderer**. He/She killed Mr. Rich.

WORD FORMS

There are several different endings which are used with words to indicate crime (noun–activity), criminal (noun–person), and action (verb). For example, a person who commits the crime of **kidnapping** is a **kidnapper**, while a person who commits the crime of **arson** is an **arsonist**. Sometimes the word doesn't change at all, as in **murder** which indicates both the action (verb) and the crime (noun). In other instances completely different words are used, as in **thief** (criminal) and **steal** (action). The following chart will help you review the words which have been used in this chapter and introduce you to some new ones. See how many you know before checking page 34 for the answers.

CRIME	CRIMINAL	ACTION (VERB)
theft	thief	steal
kidnapping		
	rapist	
arson		
	murderer	
		embezzle
burglary		
	assailant	
		forge
	robber	
		vandalize
shoplifting		
	spy	
		pick (someone's) pocket
	smuggler	

VI. EXTENSION

Consider these questions for further discussion:

1. A common English expression goes "An ounce of prevention is worth a pound of cure." In your opinion, what are the best ways to prevent crime?

2. Are all laws in your country strictly **enforced**? Should they be?

3. Are the penalties for crime in your country too tough/not tough enough?

4. Do you think that society shares part of the blame for criminal behavior?

5. Do you think that victims of crime should be compensated for their loss or suffering? If so, how and by whom?

ANSWER KEY

CRIME	CRIMINAL	ACTION (VERB)
theft	thief	steal
kidnapping	kidnapper	kidnap
rape	rapist	rape
arson	arsonist	burn (something)
murder	murderer	murder/kill
embezzlement	embezzler	embezzle
burglary	burglar	burglarize
assault	assailant	assault
forgery	forger	forge
robbery	robber	rob
vandalism	vandal	vandalize
shoplifting	shoplifter	shoplift
espionage	spy	spy
pickpocketing	pickpocket	pick (someone's) pocket
smuggling	smuggler	smuggle

CHAPTER 6

LOST IN AN UNDERGROUND CAVE

I. WARM UP

If you were lost in an underground cave, which of the following people would you like to have with you? Rank them in order of importance (most helpful = 1; least helpful = 15).

_____ geologist	_____ zoologist	_____ engineer
_____ lawyer	_____ chemist	_____ computer scientist
_____ physician	_____ botanist	_____ heavyweight boxer
_____ opera singer	_____ linguist	_____ child (7 years old)
_____ journalist	_____ mathematician	_____ business manager

Do you know what each of the above people does? Write sentences to define them.

Example: A botanist is a person who studies plant life.

A zoologist is a person who _____.

A linguist_____.

A mathematician _____.

A chemist _____.

An opera singer _____.

A geologist _____.

A journalist_____.

A physician _____.

A computer scientist _____.

An engineer _____.

A heavyweight boxer _____.

FOCUS

In this chapter, you will further develop your discussion skills while practicing relative clauses, modals and comparatives.

II. VOCABULARY PREVIEW/PRONUNCIATION

In addition to the words about occupations, these words will appear in this chapter.

crawl	injured	mushroom
footprint	tunnel	explosive
toxic	coil	crooked
rescue	gender	random
gang	perspective	sacrifice
flashlight	dynamite	get rid of
batteries	stable	chest

III. CONVERSATION STRATEGIES

In this chapter, you will practice various words and structures including modals, comparatives and relative clauses. It is assumed that you have learned these things before, so examples are given below without explanation. Ask your teacher for help if you have any trouble with them.

MODALS

The linguist **can** translate the languages. (ability)

The geologist **should** determine how stable the rocks are. (obligation)

The child **could** crawl through the passageway. (possibility)

The journalist **might** write a story about our experience in case we never get out of the cavern alive. (possibility)

COMPARATIVES

Which is **smarter**? A botanist or a zoologist?

The chemist will be **more** useful **than** the engineer because…

It's **more important to** test the air **than to** check the rocks.

RELATIVE CLAUSES

We need someone **who can lift 1,000 pounds.**

The lawyer is the only one **who can be sacrificed.**

The person **who can organize the group best** is the business manager.

OFFERING A DIFFERENT PERSPECTIVE

Sometimes you may want to bring up an idea that allows others to see things from a different point of view. To do this you may use phrases such as:

Suppose we look for some dynamite. That might be the only way out.

On the other hand, the physician is not so important if no one is injured.

Let's look at it another way. The boxer could help get rid of the snake.

Let's look at it from another viewpoint/angle. We could all get killed if this plan fails.

IV. THE SITUATION

You have been exploring an underground **cavern** with a group of tourists when you discover that you have lost your way. Nobody knows the way out and you have the feeling that you have been going around in circles for the past two hours. The group has only one **flashlight** with **batteries** which will last for only about an hour. As you quickly shine the flashlight around the large cavern, you notice the following:

1. No one has been **injured.**

2. Everyone is very hungry.

3. There is a message on the wall of the cave (approximately 25 words) written in Greek, Latin, and Hebrew.

4. In one corner, there is a patch of **mushrooms.**

5. In another corner, you see hair and **footprints** left by a large wild animal.

6. There is a large pool of water on one side of the cave, but you notice that the water level is rising at a rate of one fourth inch per minute.

7. There are five **tunnels** leading out of the cavern, but you have no idea where any of them go.

8. There is a strange smell in the air; you suspect that it is a highly **explosive** or **toxic** gas.

9. On the ground, there are a box of unused matches, a 20 meter **coil** of rope, and four gas masks.

10. There is a small opening in the ceiling, approximately 50 feet above you.

11. The opening can only be reached by a very narrow and **crooked** passageway.

12. The opening in the ceiling is covered with a sheet of glass.

13. If the glass were somehow broken, then someone with a strong voice could probably yell for help.

14. Some of the rocks in the cave walls are not very **stable**.

15. The last thing you notice is a large chest of money, probably left there by a **gang** of robbers.

16. As you walk toward the chest, you see a huge black snake coming out of it.

17. Suddenly, you hear a strange noise coming from one of the tunnels.

V. YOUR OBJECTIVE

The people of the 15 different occupations are listed below. After reading the situation with the members of your group, discuss and decide which of the people would be most useful to you. Then as a group, rank them in order of importance (most helpful = 1; least helpful = 15).

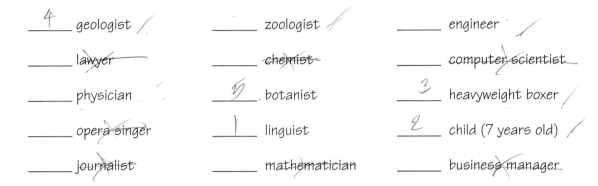

_4_ geologist

_____ lawyer

_____ physician

_____ opera singer

_____ journalist

_____ zoologist

_____ chemist

_9_ botanist

_1_ linguist

_____ mathematician

_____ engineer

_____ computer scientist

_3_ heavyweight boxer

_2_ child (7 years old)

_____ business manager

When you have finished, compare your rankings with the ones you made at the beginning of the chapter. Have you changed your mind? Why?

VI. SOMETHING TO THINK ABOUT

Suppose you were lost in a cavern with people of the fifteen occupations listed above and someone came to rescue you one at a time. Whom would you let out first?

What if you could save only five people? Which ones would you leave behind?

What factors would determine your decision?

    age
    gender
    occupation
    individual's skills
    size of a person's family
    random selection
    potential for good in society
    other

CHAPTER 7

JUST SAY NO

Match the invitation or request with an appropriate acceptance or refusal from the list on the right. There may be more than one answer for each.

Invitation/Offer/Request	Refusal
1. Would you like some more cake? _____	A. I'd rather you didn't.
2. How about some coffee? _____	B. Sorry, I have other plans.
3. Do you mind if I smoke? _____	C. I'd love to, but I can't.
4. Why don't we go swimming this weekend? _____	D. No, thanks.
5. Would you like to go to the movie with me? _____	E. Sorry, I'm not interested.
6. Here, have some whiskey. _____	F. No, but thanks for the offer.
7. Try this shrimp sauce; you'll really like it. _____	G. No. I'm afraid not.
8. Would you like a ride home? _____	H. No way.
9. Will you help me with my algebra? _____	I. I'd rather not. Thanks anyway.
10. May I have another one? _____	J. No, not really.
11. Can you help me carry these boxes? _____	K. No. Don't even think of it.
12. Just once, okay? _____	L. Sorry, I'm busy now.
13. Will you tell me the answers to the test? _____	M. I really can't. Sorry.
14. Will you type my paper for me? _____	N. Not today. How about some other time?
15. Could you do me a favor? _____	
16. Can I borrow your car? _____	Acceptance
17. If you buy it now, I'll give you a special price. _____	O. Sure.
	P. Of course.
	Q. I'd love to.
	R. Sure. I'd be glad to.
	S. Good idea.
	T. Okay. Thanks.
	U. Go ahead.
	V. Yes, please.
	W. Okay. If you insist.
	X. Sure. Why not?
	Y. No problem.
	Z. Sounds good.

ANSWER KEY

Listed below are the best answers to the matching exercise on the previous page. If you have questions about other acceptable answers, ask your teacher or a native speaker of English for help.

1. D, F, T, V	7. D, T	13. G, H, O*, W*
2. D, F, T	8. D, F, O	14. L, M, O, R, Y
3. A, U	9. M, N, O, R	15. G, L, M, R, Y
4. B, C, I, L, N, O, Q	10. A, G, O, P, U, X	16. A, H, U, Y
5. C, I, L, N, O, Q	11. G, M, O, R, Y	17. E, T, Z
6. D, I, T, M	12. H, K, M, X, W	

*While these may be linguistically correct, they are not recommended in this situation.

FOCUS

The phrases presented in the Warm Up exercise give you some useful ways to extend and accept or turn down invitations or requests. In this chapter, you will practice saying no politely in various situations.

II. VOCABULARY PREVIEW

Listed below are some words and expressions introduced in this chapter.

rapport	tactic	reinforce
persistent	overbearing	marijuana
illegal	convince	persuade
vegetarian	forbid	choir
insignificant	shrimp	sauce
misunderstanding	algebra	sundae
customary	parrot	pretzel
run (an) errand	egg (someone) on	be allergic to (something)

III. CONVERSATION STRATEGIES

SMALL TALK/GREETINGS

If you haven't seen someone for a while, it is good to first greet them and make small talk for a minute or two before asking them to do something. For example,

> A: Kelly, how you doing?
>
> B: Okay, I guess. How's everything with you?
>
> A: Can't complain. I just took my last final this morning.
>
> B: Me too. It's good to have them over with.
>
> A: Say, do you know about the Jane Elton concert next Friday?
>
> B: Yes, I've heard about it.
>
> A: Well I was wondering if...

A few informal greetings are listed below

How (are) you doing?	How have you been?
How ya doing?	What's up (What are you doing?)
How's everything?	What have you been up to?
How's it going?	(What have you been doing recently?)

GETTING TO THE POINT/INVITING

It is usually not polite to talk for a long time about **insignificant** things. The other person may have other things to do and may feel small talk is a waste of his/her time. It is important to bring up the subject as soon as you have established a good rapport with your partner. Some phrases for doing this are listed below.

INVITATIONS

There's a dance at the Rotunda Center this Friday. **Would you like to go?**

I was wondering if you would like to go to the game with me on Saturday.

How would you like to go out for an ice cream sundae?

OFFERS

Would you like a cookie/**some** more soup?

How about a glass of wine/some pretzels?

Can I get you something to drink?

REQUESTS

Could you do me a favor?

Would you mind if I asked you something/a personal question?

Is it okay if I leave my parrot here for the weekend?

ADDED ENCOURAGEMENT

People may use various **tactics** to encourage or persuade you to go along with them after you have initially refused. This is called "egging on." Listed below are some common phrases used to egg someone on as well as some phrases for refusing the additional persuasion.

<u>EGGING ON:</u>

Everybody else is going.

C'mon. One time won't hurt.

What's wrong with a little bit?

You'll miss all the fun.

<u>TURNING DOWN:</u>

Sorry, I just can't.

When I say "no" I mean NO.

I'd really rather not.

Thanks anyway. I'll pass.

CONFIRMING APPOINTMENTS

After an invitation has been extended and accepted, it is good to confirm the date and time before closing the conversation. This **reinforces** the commitment and ensures that there are no **misunderstandings**. It is also a friendly way to say good-bye. Some common phrases for doing this are listed below.

See you on Friday at 7.

Okay, I'll pick you up Saturday at 5:30.

I'll call and let you know the time.

IV. YOUR OBJECTIVE

In this activity you will extend an invitation to your partner to do something which he or she doesn't particularly want to do. Your partner will refuse the first time. Try to persuade your partner to change his/her mind. Be **persistent** but not **overbearing**. If your partner really doesn't want to do what you propose, back off or change the subject. Don't risk destroying your friendship.

Role play the following situations with a partner. Remember to use the expressions you learned in the Warm Up exercise. Your teacher will monitor the time and tell you when to change partners.

V. TheSITUATIONS

1. A. Invite your partner to go dancing this weekend.
   B. You're not interested in dancing.

   _____

2. A: Try to get your partner to smoke **marijuana**.
   B. You do not want to take any kind of drug.

   _____

3. A. Ask your partner if you can borrow his/her bicycle
   B. You need the bicycle to run some **errands**.

   _____

4. A: Offer your partner a slice of ham.
   B. You are a **vegetarian**.

   _____

5. A: Offer your partner some wine.
   B. Your religion **forbids** drinking alcohol.

   _____

6. A: Ask your partner to help with your homework.
   B. You're too busy right now.

   _____

7. A: Try to get your partner to have another piece of pie.
   B. You're on a diet.

   _____

8. A: Try to sell your partner something he/she doesn't want.
   B. You're not at all interested in the product.

9. A: Ask your partner to take you to the airport.

B. You're tired of being a "taxi driver."

_____

10. A: See if your partner will get you a 20% discount on an item from his company.

B. The company doesn't give discounts except to its own employees.

_____

11. A: Invite your partner to watch home videos with you tonight.

B. You had planned on a romantic evening with your boyfriend/girlfriend.

_____

12. A: Ask your partner to join your church choir.

B. You hate to sing.

_____

13. A: Offer your partner a dish of your "famous" seafood salad.

B. You are **allergic** to seafood.

_____

14. A: Ask your partner to stay for "a couple more drinks."

B. You must get back home to study for a big test tomorrow.

_____

VI. SOMETHING TO THINK ABOUT

Discuss these questions as a class:

1. If a person says "no" once, does he/she really mean it, or does he/she expect you to ask again?

2. Have you ever been persuaded to do something you didn't want to do?

3. Do you think some people need to be pushed/encouraged before they will do something?

4. Have you ever convinced someone to do something against his/her wishes?

CHAPTER 8

GETTING THE WORD OUT

I. WARM UP

Discuss these questions as a class:

1. Is advertising a good, bad or a necessary evil?

2. What are its benefits/costs to **consumers**?

3. What are its benefits/costs to business people?

4. How are you influenced by magazine/newspaper ads?

5. What are some creative ways to get **publicity** for your company/organization?

FOCUS

In this chapter, you will learn strategies for discussing and presenting your views on a given topic (advertising). You will also have a chance to create a television commercial with your group.

II. VOCABULARY PREVIEW/PRONUNCIATION

consumer	commercial	publicity
optimal	capacity	durable
flexible	lightweight	versatile
cavity	snack	cholesterol
market	consult	concede
highlight	withstand	fabric
superior	quench	bond
wear and tear	obnoxious	prior
come up with	zipper	heavy duty
put all your eggs in one basket	merit	stain

III. CONVERSATION STRATEGIES

SETTING UP A DISCUSSION

In order to make the best use of time, it is good to focus the discussion and keep it on topic. These phrases can be used to introduce agenda items or get a discussion going :

To begin with, we need to consider how each of these ideas will affect sales.
Let's start by doing a cost/benefit analysis.

CONCEDING TO MAKE A POINT

One way to make a point without being **obnoxious** is to first **concede** (admit that you may be wrong) then state your idea. For example:

I may be wrong, but I think that's way too much for a few seconds on TV.
Correct me if I'm wrong, but shouldn't we consult the boss first?

You may be right, but isn't it better to spend less on magazine ads and more on brochures that we can send directly to potential clients?
That idea has merits, but the bottom line is price.

USING MODALS FOR MAKING SUGGESTIONS

Modals such as *could* and *might* can soften an otherwise bold statement. Note the differences in the sentences below:

We **should** put $5,000 into newspaper ads. (strong)
We **could** put $5,000 into newspaper ads. (more like a suggestion)

We **must** sponsor a huge community event. (very strong)
We **might** consider sponsoring a huge community event. (suggestion)

PRESENTATION STRATEGIES

In Chapter 4, you learned some techniques for organizing a presentation. When you make a statement and then give reasons or details to back it up, you are using the **topic/support** method. This method can be used for your presentation here.

A sample outline is given below:

Statement: Our committee/group decided to divide the budget between

_____ and _____.

Support: We chose _____ because...

We will invest $_____ in this type of advertising.

Support: We decided on _____ because...

We plan to put $_____ into it.

IV. THE SITUATION

Your company is going to open a branch in a large city with a potential **market** of two million customers. First, choose a product or service to market, then decide how to advertise it. You have an advertising budget of $100,000 to divide up any way you wish. Be careful not to **put all your eggs in one basket.**

V. YOUR OBJECTIVE

Listed on the next page are various methods of advertising. Discuss all the options with your group, and decide how much, if anything, you will spend on each. It is wise to spread your budget among different types of advertising because you want to reach a wide variety of people. The key is to spend an **optimal** amount (not too much and not too little) on each type of advertising you choose.

Discuss the advantages and disadvantages of the following options with your group and prepare a presentation on the method or methods you think are best. Your teacher will call on one of the members of your group to present your conclusions.

Our product:

Our target market:

Our advertising plan:

POSSIBLE METHODS OF ADVERTISING:

1. Newspaper ads/Print media
   > advantages
   > disadvantages
   > amount to spend

2. Television/Radio commercials
   > advantages
   > disadvantages
   > amount to spend

3. Direct mail
   > advantages
   > disadvantages
   > amount to spend

4. Billboards
   > advantages
   > disadvantages
   > amount to spend

6. Internet web site
   > advantages
   > disadvantages
   > amount to spend

7. Posters/Flyers
   > advantages
   > disadvantages
   > amount to spend

8. Trade shows/Exhibitions
   > advantages
   > disadvantages
   > amount to spend

9. Other ideas
   > advantages
   > disadvantages
   > amount to spend

VI. EXTENSION

In this activity, you will have a chance to be creative as you and the members of your group produce and present a television commercial for your product.

The best way to organize your information is to think of features of the product and why they are important. For example:

PRODUCT: ZIPPO PLASTIC BAGS	
FEATURE	WHY IS THIS IMPORTANT?
4 quart **capacity**	can store more food
durable	will last longer
resistant to cold temperatures	can **withstand** low temperatures
flexible	can stretch to hold more
lightweight	easy to hold and transport

Zippo plastic bags have a four quart capacity, so you can store a lot a food.
*They are durable, so you don't have to worry about **wear and tear**.*

Also, be sure to **highlight** special parts of the product.

For example: *press–tight seal*

The press–tight seal allows you to lock in the food's freshness.

COMMONLY USED PASSIVE CONSTRUCTIONS

Sometimes the passive voice is used to describe products and their features. Some common passive constructions are as follows:

It is made of durable stainless steel.
It was made in Germany.
It is used for oven cleaning.
It was designed by scientists **for** home use.
It is recommended by Dr. Bill **for** an upset stomach.
It is equipped with a plastic spout for pouring.

MAKING TELEVISION COMMERCIALS

PROBLEM/SOLUTION

An easy way to make a TV advertisement is to present a problem and then offer your product as the ideal solution. For example, you might bring up the problem with a question:

Are you tired of dirty spots on your laundry?

Have you ever noticed how bright some people's teeth are?

Are you looking for a low-calorie afternoon snack?

Show how your product is the best solution to the problem. You might use phrases like these:

Handy-Dandy does the job of ten wrenches.

Glisteen toothpaste makes your smile shine.

With *EatLight-EatRight*, you'll never worry about gaining weight again.

SPOTLIGHT

Another way is to focus on a new feature of the product and show how this feature makes your product **superior** to others or makes it essential for customers to buy.

Now you can get your clothes their whitest with *Expo*.

Lite-n-Soft's **heavy duty** zippers will never let you down.

BANDWAGON EFFECT

Another method of advertising is to make consumers believe that everyone else is using your product, and that to be a part of the group, they should use it too.

Pop City cola: the taste everybody's talking about.

It's about time you joined the *Crispo* crowd.

Multimacho vitamins: Healthy people use them; shouldn't you?

Use your imagination and see what else you can **come up with**.

VII. THE ACTIVITY

With your group, create a television commercial for ONE of the following products:

1. *Expo* laundry detergent

   gets clothes cleaner than the leading brand

   no damage to **fabrics**

2. *Multimacho* vitamins

   recommended by doctors

   delicious, kids love them

3. *Glisteen* toothpaste

   extra white teeth

   fights cavities

4. *Crispo* potato chips

   excellent for afternoon snacks

   low **cholesterol**, no salt

5. *Stick–Up* glue

   bonds anything to anything

   special offer: buy one, get one free

6. *Pop City* soda

   quenches your thirst in a hurry

   tastes better than other brands

7. *Lite–n–Soft* jacket

   many pockets

   heavy duty zipper

8. *Handy–Dandy* wrench

   versatile

   strong

   multipurpose

9. Your own product

   feature:

   feature:

CHAPTER 9

MAKE ME A MATCH

I. WARM UP

Pre-discussion questions:

In your home country, do parents choose mates for their children?

Did they in "the olden days"?

Do you think romantic love is a good **criterion** for choosing a spouse?

Should money and social **status** be important factors in choosing a husband/wife?

Do you think **traditions** are important and should be kept?

What do you think of the statement, "You don't marry an individual, you marry into a family"?

Focus

In this chapter, you will practice sales English vocabulary and expressions as you go "shopping" for a spouse for one of your clients.

II. VOCABULARY PREVIEW/PRONUNCIATION

prospective	status	initiate
tradition	client	brochure
agent	firm (noun)	profile
courtship	enlist	commission
treat	potential	interracial
candidate	narrow down	shortcoming
criterion	intently	superlative
reassure	enhance	dessert

Additional vocabulary words will be given in the activity section of this chapter.

III. THE SITUATION

You have a 29 year old son and a 25 year old daughter. Both are college–educated and have good jobs with large international **firms**. They have also traveled extensively and both speak three languages. While they are quite successful in most areas of life, neither has time for **courtship** and marriage. Naturally, as a parent you are quite concerned. It bothers you to see them alone so much, and more importantly, you would like some grandchildren before you die. You **enlist** the help of a computer dating service. After six weeks of waiting for a reply, you receive several written **profiles** of prospective spouses in the mail.

In this activity, your classmates will play the roles of agents looking for **prospective** spouses for their clients. Each agent will receive a large **commission** if he/she matches your son/daughter up with his/her **client**.

IV. YOUR OBJECTIVE

Your objectives will be different depending on whether you are a parent or an agent.

As a parent, your objective is to find the best wife for your son or best husband for your daughter. Ask careful questions of each of the agents. Find out as much information as you can about prospective spouses before making any commitments.

As an agent, your objective is to find the best partner for your client. There are only six parents in the exercise. If your client is not suitable for any of them, try doing business with the other agents. Try to match your client with one of theirs.

PROCEDURE

Walk around the room talking to as many agents as you can to find out information about prospective spouses for your son or daughter. After you have narrowed it down to a few, you can always go back and ask more questions. Be creative. You may fill in/make up details as you go along.

CHARACTERS IN THE ROLE PLAY

Your teacher will assign you one of the following roles:

Parent 1 (daughter)	Agent for Mr. A	Agent for Mr. G
Parent 2 (son)	Agent for Miss B	Agent for Miss H
Parent 3 (daughter)	Agent for Mr. C	Agent for Mr. I
Parent 4 (son)	Agent for Miss D	Agent for Miss J
Parent 5 (daughter)	Agent for Mr. E	Agent for Mr. K
Parent 6 (son)	Agent for Miss F	Agent for Miss L

Carefully look over the information in the "Profiles of Prospective Mates" section to get an idea of whom you represent (as an agent). If you are a "parent," look over all the profiles and determine which agent you would like to talk to first.

V. CONVERSATION STRATEGIES

In this activity, the parents act as "customers" and the agents as "salespeople." The formalities of sales English depend in part on who approaches whom.

For example, if the **customer** approaches the salesperson, he/she might say something like:

> Hi. **I'm looking for** a tablecloth for my kitchen.
> husband for my daughter.
> **Excuse me, could you tell me a little about** these sandals?
> Ms. B?
> **Could you give me some background/information on** Mr. C?

If the **customer** approaches first but doesn't say anything, the salesperson might initiate a conversation with

> **What can I do for you?**
> **May I help you?**

If the salesperson and customer have made an appointment, the **salesperson** might open a conversation with

> **I understand you are looking for** a pool table
> a partner for your son/daughter.
> **So, you're in the market for** a motor home.

After listening intently to the customer's response, the **salesperson** might say

> **Perhaps I could interest you in** this silverware set.
> one of my clients.
> **I have just the** woman/man **for you.**
> Let me tell you a little about my client.
> **As you can see from the** profile/**brochure**, Mr. E is an excellent candidate.

The salesperson and customer will then discuss details. The salesperson can use **superlative** phrases like:

> Mr. G is **one of the** bright**est** clients I have.
> Ms. D is **one of the best** cooks I've ever met.
> Mr. I is **the nicest guy** on the list.

Customers should be sure to ask as many questions as possible to find out what they can about the person's character, interests, **shortcomings**, etc. For example:

> Can she drive?
> Does he play football?
> What does she do for a living?
> Has he been married before?

As a customer, feel free to raise any concerns you might have. For example:

> What about his family? How will they treat my daughter?
> I'm a little concerned about his drinking.
> How does she deal with conflict?
> Could you give me more details about...?

Salespeople should **reassure** customers that their client is the best choice. If a customer raises a negative point, they should contrast it with a positive one:

> A: I'm looking for a woman with a lot of musical talent.
> B: Ms. F may not know how to sing, **but** she really can dance.

> A: Is Mr. K athletic?
> B: **Not really, but** he does weight lifting twice a week.

Be sure to add relevant details to **enhance** your client's image:

> Ms. D is an excellent cook. **In fact,** she won a blue ribbon (first place award) for her homemade desserts.
> **As a matter of fact,** Mr. E loves horseback riding.
> **Actually,** Ms. H doesn't need a car. She takes the subway to work.

PROFILES OF PROSPECTIVE MATES

MR. A

Health: *good*

Occupation: *college professor*

Money: *$50,000 in bonds*

Best attribute: *well-read on many subjects*

Worst attribute: *snobbish*

Education: *Ph.D. in philosophy*

Talents: *public speaking, cooking*

Hobbies: *reading professional journals*

Idea of a great date: *going to a symphony*

MR. C

Health: *gets sick often*

Occupation: *rock singer*

Money: *millionaire*

Best attribute: *generous with money*

Worst attribute: *alcoholic, womanizer*

Education: *high school dropout*

Talents: *singing, performing*

Hobbies: *skydiving, race car driving*

Idea of a great date: *watching his own concerts on videotape*

MR. E

Health: *excellent*

Occupation: *electrical engineer*

Money: *barely makes ends meet*

Best attribute: *very intelligent*

Worst attribute: *insensitive to others*

Education: *M.S. in physics*

Talents: *computer whiz*

Hobbies: *travel, racquetball*

Idea of a great date: *pizza and videos*

MS. B

Health: *very good*

Occupation: *civil engineer*

Money: *$60,000 in savings*

Best attribute: *thrifty*

Worst attribute: *stubborn*

Education: *M.S. mathematics*

Talents: *analytical skills*

Hobbies: *hiking, camping*

Idea of a great date: *nature walks*

MS. D

Health: *good*

Occupation: *secretary*

Money: *$2,000 in debt*

Best attribute: *kind-hearted*

Worst attribute: *naive*

Education: *vocational school*

Talents: *clarinet and trumpet*

Hobbies: *waterskiing, swimming*

Idea of a great date: *going bowling*

MS. F

Health: *poor*

Occupation: *doctor*

Money: *still paying off loans*

Best attribute: *confident*

Worst attribute: *bossy*

Education: *M.D.*

Talents: *handicrafts*

Hobbies: *sculpture, painting*

Idea of a great date: *a day on her yacht*

MR. G

Health: very good
Occupation: auto mechanic
Money: no disposable income
Best attribute: easy–going, romantic
Worst attribute: doesn't plan for future
Education: B.S. in psychology
Talents: mechanical things
Hobbies: scuba diving
Idea of a great date: evening at the
health spa

MR. I

Health: poor
Occupation: plumber
Money: $5,000 in savings
Best attribute: flexible, caring nature
Worst attribute: not self–motivated
Education: B.S. economics
Talents: can fix anything
Hobbies: stamp collecting
Idea of a great date: fast food and a movie

MR. K

Health: crippled, but otherwise healthy
Occupation: stock broker
Money: millions in stocks and bonds
Best attribute: very practical
Worst attribute: impatient
Education: MBA
Talents: business skills
Hobbies: wheelchair basketball
Idea of a great date: watching the city
lights from afar

MS. H

Health: excellent
Occupation: disk jockey
Money: $3,000 in savings
Best attribute: great sense of humor
Worst attribute: absent–minded
Education: B.A. in art
Talents: people skills
Hobbies: going to parties
Idea of a great date: night club entertainment

MS. J

Health: very good
Occupation: model
Money: makes and spends a lot
Best attribute: good physique
Worst attribute: emotionally immature
Education: high school diploma
Talents: acting, gymnastics
Hobbies: shopping, aerobics
Idea of a great date: suntanning on the beach

MS. L

Health: very good
Occupation: author
Money: very wealthy parents
Best attribute: cultured, smart
Worst attribute: self–centered
Education: M.A. in communications
Talents: plays the piano
Hobbies: knitting, handicrafts
Idea of a great date: afternoon in
the library

VI. SOMETHING TO THINK ABOUT

Be prepared to discuss these questions as a class:

1. In your opinion, how important are "good looks" in selecting a **potential** mate?

2. If someone asks you how to go about finding a suitable marriage partner, what will you tell him/her?

3. If your parents chose a marriage partner for you, what would you do?

4. Do you think it is all right for people to remain single for their whole lives if they choose to do so?

5. What do you think parents should do if their children are not interested in people of the opposite sex?

6. What about race? Is it a factor in your selection of a marriage partner? What are your opinions about **interracial** marriage?

CHAPTER 10

PARENTAL PUNISHMENT

I. WARM UP

Do you **agree** or **disagree** with the following statements?

1. Punishing children is an act of love.
2. Little girls should never be punished physically.
3. Parents should stop **spanking** when their children are eight years old.
4. Parents should never lay a hand on a child.
5. Psychological punishment can be just as **severe** as physical punishment.
6. It is okay to **humiliate** a child in front of his/her friends.
7. If children are not punished for wrongdoing, they will never learn.
8. The wrong kind of **discipline** is better than no discipline at all.

FOCUS

In this chapter, you will learn strategies for giving and receiving feedback as well as phrases for expressing cause and effect.

II. VOCABULARY PREVIEW/PRONUNCIATION

spank	severe	humiliate
discipline	jail	candy bar
subtle	strict	lenient
curfew	chore	disobey
confinement	guilty	restitution
consequence	privilege	withhold
allowance	alcoholic	mood
restrain	stern	grounding
grab	slap	expel
recess	swear	abrupt

III. CONVERSATION STRATEGIES

SHOWING OBLIGATION

The words *should, need to, ought to, had better, have to, have got to,* and *must* are used to express requirement or obligation. The differences are very subtle. They are listed below from least serious to most serious.

		MEANING
Bruce	**needs to** go to his room.	He is required to do it
Bruce	**ought to**	It would be a good idea.
	should	It is important that he does it.
	had better	If he doesn't, something bad will happen.
	has to	Someone demands that he do it.
	has got to	He cannot hesitate.
	must	Absolutely.

In a discussion, there are certain expressions used to get and give feedback. Some of the most common are:

ASKING FOR FEEDBACK

Are you following me?
Are you with me so far?
Have you got that?

EXPRESSING CONFUSION/LACK OF UNDERSTANDING

I don't understand.
I didn't quite catch that.
What do you mean by… ?
What was that again?

CONFIRMATION OF COMPREHENSION

I see.
I understand.
Gotcha. (informal)

SHOWING POSSIBLE CONSEQUENCES

Marla should quit drinking, **or** she might become an alcoholic.

I had better be home by nine; **otherwise**, I will be grounded for a week.

Give it back, **or else!** (implied negative consequences)

GIVING THE REASON

Compare the usage of **because**, **since**, and **so**.

Johnny should be punished **because** he disobeyed.

Because he disobeyed, Johnny should be punished.

Since he disobeyed, Johnny should be punished.

Johnny disobeyed, **so** he should be punished.

Just because is used to single out a particular reason.

Just because he stole one candy bar, it doesn't mean he will become a lifetime thief.

Just because I was late for school, my mother won't let me use the car for a week.

MATTER

The word *matter* is used in many contexts. For example,

What's the matter? (What wrong?/What's the problem?)

It doesn't matter. (It is not important.)

When *it doesn't matter* is used to introduce another idea, it is usually follow by *if* or *a wh–question word*.

It doesn't matter **if** it was an accident; he should still pay for the window.

It doesn't matter **where** you went; you disobeyed.

The same holds true for *no matter*.

No matter what he says, he is still guilty.

I'm in deep trouble **no matter when** I get home.

The special expression, *no matter what*, when used abruptly at the end of a sentence, means "there is no alternative."

She should be grounded, **no matter what!**

NO WONDER

When used at the beginning of a clause or sentence, *no wonder* means "It's not surprising that… "

> **No wonder** he's in jail now; his parents always let him run wild as a child.
> **No wonder** she has ten cavities; she never brushes her teeth.

EVEN IF

Some students use *even* by itself as a subordinator. When used to pinpoint a particular condition, *even* should be followed by *if*. For example:

> **Even** I tell them the truth, my parents will get angry. INCORRECT
> **Even if** I tell them the truth, my parents will get angry.

HAVE/MAKE VERSUS ASK/TELL

There are several ways to indicate that you want another person to do something. Notice the difference in both structure and meaning:

(I would) **have** him **pay** for the damages.	(firm)
(I would) **make** him **clean** up the mess.	(forceful)
(I think we should) **ask** her **to apologize**.	(mild)
(I think we should) **tell** her **not to do** it again.	(stronger)

IV. THE SITUATION

Parents are often faced with tough choices in disciplining their children. Some parents may be very **strict**, others quite **lenient**. How would you deal with a child who misbehaves? In small groups, discuss the following situations and decide on the appropriate punishment. You may select from the choices at the bottom of the page or come up with your own.

Discuss openly; this is not a role play.

1. Johnny, 6, is caught playing with matches

2. Cathy, 15, comes home after **curfew**

3. Todd, 5, steals a **candy bar** from the grocery store

4. Brenda, 7, talks back to her parents

5. Keith, 11, doesn't do his homework

6. Carrie, 13, cheats on a test

7. Scott, 8, gets into a fight with another boy

8. Rosalie, 14, takes drugs

9. Karl, 12, doesn't do his **chores**

10. Holly, 4, doesn't eat her vegetables

11. Trent, 9, throws a rock through a neighbor's window

12. Ivy, 10, hurts another girl's feelings

13. Chad, 7, punches another boy in the nose

14. Mindy, 8, tells a lie

CHOICES OF PUNISHMENT		
Nothing	Yelling/Using a stern voice	Taking away privileges
Spanking	Humiliating/Embarrassing	Assigning extra chores
Grounding	Allowing natural consequences	Expressing disappointment
Shaming	Withholding allowance	Using the "silent treatment"
Restraining	Confining child to room	(Ignoring the child)

Making the   child apologize
sit in a corner
feel guilty
repair damaged items
pay compensation
stay home from an activity

V. FOLLOW UP

Consider the questions below and be prepared to share your opinions in a class discussion.

1. What should be the determining factors for using physical punishment to discipline a child?

   age of the child

   sex of the child

   seriousness of the offense

   mood of the parent

2. What do you think about physical punishment in schools?

   Does the teacher have a right to hit or restrain students when they misbehave?

3. Which of these punishments do you feel are appropriate in the classroom?

   hitting with a ruler

   grabbing an arm, shoulder or ear to restrain a child

   slapping

   calling the principal

   informing the parents

   making students stay in the room during recess

   making the students stay after school

   having students stand silently for long periods of time

   yelling at students

   swearing

   assigning extra homework

   expelling from school

   sending home a note for the parents to sign

   lowering grades

   other

CHAPTER 11

IT'S YOUR CHOICE

Suppose you and a two of your **colleagues** have been taken **hostage** in a room on the thirteenth floor of a high-rise office building. A **gunman** is pointing his **pistol** at you. He starts threatening you with words like

Don't move or I'll shoot!

With his words, the gunman is giving you a simple choice. (Stay put or die.) He could also express the same idea using other words:

If you move, I will shoot.
If you don't move, I will not shoot.

Phrases like these carry a lot of power (not to mention the key to your staying alive in this situation.) They fulfill two functions at the same time:

1) They offer a clear choice

Choice A: *You move.*
Choice B: *You don't move.*

2) They indicate the consequences of one choice and imply the consequences of the other.

Consequence A: *I will shoot.*
Consequence B: *I will not shoot.*

In this chapter, you will learn to use **"if" statements** to express present choices and their future consequences.

NOTE: Vocabulary is provided as a review at the end of the chapter.

II. CONVERSATION STRATEGIES

IF STATEMENTS

PRESENT CHOICE/FUTURE CONSEQUENCE

The easiest of the **if statements** to understand is the **present choice** and **future consequence**. These statements express a simple choice and a possible outcome.

> If you move, I'll **shoot**!
> If you eat too much candy, you **will get** sick.
> If you don't call your mother, she **will get** upset.

Also

> If you **eat** your broccoli, you **can have** some ice cream.

Since each of these involves a slightly different approach, they will be dealt with separately in this chapter.

III. THE SITUATIONS

The following situations will give you opportunities to use **if statements** in conversation. Practice them with a partner. Try to put them in the context of a real dialogue.

For the first set, use the pattern, **If (present tense), (future tense).**

> **Example:**

> Situation: You are driving too fast. You must slow down or you will get a speeding ticket.

> > A: How fast are you going?
> > B: About 65. Why do you ask?
> > A: We just passed a sign that says "Speed Limit 45."
> > B: I didn't see it. I guess I should slow down a little.
> > A: You'd better. **If you don't slow down, that policeman will give you a ticket.**
> > B: Oh, I didn't see him either.

Practice these situations with a partner:

1. You are eating a lot of chocolate cake. Your partner warns you about getting sick.

2. Your partner never exercises. Warn him/her about gaining weight.

3. Your puppy has a near fatal disease. You'd better take him to the veterinarian soon. (If you don't take him to the veterinarian…)

4. George is standing on the ledge of a tall building. He has just proposed to Martha. Martha hasn't answered yet. George is ready to jump if her answer is no.

5. Melvin is very lazy and refuses to get a job. Clara, his wife, threatens to leave him. (Use third person here; for example: "If Melvin doesn't get a job…")

6. It is midnight and the teenagers are playing loud music. The next-door neighbor, Mrs. Crabby threatens to call the police.

7. Your partner owns a small grocery store, but has very few customers. Most people shop at Wally's, where the prices are lower. Advise your partner. (Try: If you lower your prices…")

NOTE: When talking about another person, use third-person singular. For example:
> If you **don't get** a job, I'll leave.
> If he **doesn't get** a job, she will leave. (third person singular)

WHAT IF

The question **what if** allows you to explore your options further:

> A: **What if** I don't sign these papers?
> B: If you don't sign, you won't get paid.
>
> A: **What if** she says no?
> B: Then find someone else.

PERMISSION

Can and **may** are used in these types of statements to show that the outcome is dependent on a person's being allowed or receiving permission to do something.

Example:

> Mom says **if** we clean our rooms, we **can/may** go to the movie.
> **If** she quits her job, she **can** spend more time with the kids.

For the next set of situations, use *can* or **may** in place of *will*.

1. It is New Year's Eve. The boss will allow anyone who finishes their work to go home early. (If you finish your work on time...)

2. You might make a trip to Kentucky. Your uncle will let you stay in his house so you don't have to stay in a hotel.

3. You don't have enough money for the computer right now. The **clerk** will allow you to pay in **installments**.

4. Your teacher will let you do a term project instead of taking the final exam. (You will be able to **waive** the final exam.)

5. You can't decide whether to go to Tahiti or Rome on your next vacation. Discuss the types of activities you can do in each location. (If I go to Tahiti...)

6. You want to run for **mayor** of your community. You know that there is a lot of **hassle** associated with the job, but you also see many benefits and opportunities.

7. You wonder if you should "call in sick" today. You feel **miserable**, but you have a lot of work to finish before the weekend. What will happen if you stay home? What if you don't?

IV. EXTENSION ACTIVITY

If **statements** come in handy when you must choose from many options. For example, if you are selecting a restaurant, you might discuss the various possibilities. See how they are used in the dialogue below.

A: Where should we go for dinner tonight?
B: Well, it depends. If you are in the mood for Chinese food, we can eat at the Golden Dragon.
A: Yes, but if we go there, it will take us half an hour (travel time).
B: We can go to Tio Paco's. It's right around the corner.
A: Can't we go somewhere cheaper?
B: If you like fast food, we can go to McDougal's
A: No, I'd rather have pizza.
B: Well, if you don't make up your mind soon, we will starve...

With your partner or group, decide on the best restaurant for dinner. Choose from the options below or from local restaurants in your area.

McDougal's
Type of restaurant: Fast food
Distance from home: 5 blocks
Average cost of a meal: $5.95
Atmosphere: noisy
Special features: boxed meals for kids

Tio Paco's
Type of restaurant: Mexican
Distance: around the corner
Average cost of a meal: $21
Atmosphere: fun, lively
Special features: live music

The Steak Center
Type of restaurant: buffet
Distance: 6 miles away
Average cost of a meal: $15
Atmosphere: cozy, pleasant
Special features: all-you-can-eat salad bar

The Golden Dragon
Type of restaurant: Chinese
Distance from home: 20 miles
Average cost of a meal: $29
Atmosphere: comfortable
Special features: Hong Kong chef

Pierre's
Type of restaurant: French
Distance: 7 miles away
Average cost of a meal: $45
Atmosphere: sophisticated
Special features: candlelight

Jake's Cakes
Type of restaurant: coffee shop
Distance: 3 miles (at the mall)
Average cost of a meal: $9
Atmosphere: friendly
Special features: free coffee refills

V. VOCABULARY REVIEW

hostage	pistol	gunman
fatal	veterinarian	ledge
installments	miserable	mayor
outcome	hassle	mall
cancel	clerk	broccoli
waive	buffet	sophisticated
handy	atmosphere	chef
colleague	cozy	starve
teenager	propose	call in sick

CHAPTER 12

GETTING DOWN TO BUSINESS

As the owner of a business, which of the following do you think is most important? Rank from 1 to 12. (1 = most important; 12 = least important)

_____ Making a profit

_____ Serving the community

_____ Providing benefits for employees

_____ Keeping a good name in the community

_____ Holding a large share of the market

_____ Increasing value of company stock

_____ Maintaining good relationships with customers

_____ Having good connections with government officials

_____ Beating the competition

_____ Keeping expenses low

_____ Maintaining company assets

_____ Staying out of debt

FOCUS

In this chapter, you will use English to analyze a business situation and make recommendations. You may wish to review the discussion and presentation strategies of Chapters 4 and 8.

II. CONVERSATION STRATEGIES

ANALYZING A SITUATION

Business analysis and case studies involve looking at a situation and discussing how it might be improved or how it could have been handled better in the past.

First, **investigate** the situation thoroughly to be sure that you understand the main problems to be discussed.

After looking over the data, you may need to draw temporary conclusions. Here are some phrases for doing so:

> It appears that...
>
> It looks like...
>
> The problem here is...
>
> Part of the problem is...

FOCUSING ON ONE ISSUE

You may wish to concentrate the discussion on one major issue. Some phrases for doing this are

> The real issue is...
>> main point
>> question
>
> What's important is...

GETTING IMMEDIATE ANSWERS

> What I want to (wanna) know is...
> What are we going to (gonna) do about it?

OUTLINING PLANS FOR ACTION

> There are several things that can be done.
>
> The first step is to...
>
> Another thing is...

MAKING RECOMMENDATIONS

When **recommend** is followed by **that** and a clause, a special type of grammar is used:

I would like to **recommend that** subject + simple verb

Example

I **recommend that** she *pay* for the damages. (not *pays*)

I **recommend that** you *go* to the convention.

He **recommends that** I *see* a psychiatrist.

I **would like to recommend that** he *be* suspended. (not *is*)

PRESENTING YOUR RECOMMENDATIONS

To show that you have studied the situation thoroughly, you may introduce your recommendations with phrases such as:

After carefully reviewing the situation, we came to the following conclusions:

Based on the results of our investigation, we would like to make these recommendations:

1. _____

_____

2. _____

_____

3. _____

_____

4. _____

_____

III. SITUATION

The Maze Corporation is losing business in one section of the metropolitan area. Sales have gone down **dramatically** during the past six months in its West Suburbia department store. The board of directors can't figure out why, because their store in East Suburbia is **thriving**. An evaluation team visited the West Suburbia store last week to **analyze** the situation. These are the things they found:

1.	Location	Seaside Mall in West Suburbia **Inaccessible** by public transportation
2.	Management	General manager spends his days at the country club
3.	Employee **Morale**	**Contention** among employees
4.	Employee Benefits	Expensive health **insurance** Poorly run day care center
5.	Market	Mostly low-income families Upper class is moving out of neighborhood
6.	Customer Satisfaction	Complaints of rudeness and poor treatment by employees Some clerks ignore customers
7.	Taxes	30% of profits Extremely high sales tax
8.	**Overhead**	Low rent High **utilities** cost
9.	**Maintenance**	**Leaky** roof Lazy **custodian**
10.	Sales **Volume**	Down—except in Sporting Goods, Toys, and Infants Departments
11.	Competition	Valley Mart is **luring** away customers with its discount prices
12.	Promotions	Seasonal (Christmas, Back-to-School, Valentine's Day sales) Annual $25,000 prize **lottery**
13.	Advertisement	Newspaper **inserts** Discount **coupons**
14.	Charge Accounts	Too many **overdue** accounts
15.	Dishonesty	Customers: Shoplifting Employees: Embezzlement, falsely reporting work hours
16.	**Bureaucracy**	Lots of paper work Employees spend too much time on reports
17.	Suppliers	**Distributors** are slow in filling orders
18.	Community Service	Huge **contribution** to the Thanksgiving Day parade. Sponsorship of a new **auditorium** and **gymnasium** for the local high school
19.	Entertainment	Wining and dining government officials
20.	Law suit	A customer slipped on the wet floor, **twisted** her ankle and is **suing** for $1 million in damages.

IV. YOUR OBJECTIVE

You and the members of your group are part of an evaluation team from **headquarters** and must make recommendations on what to do about the West Suburbia store. You realize that you cannot fix everything at once but must focus on the most important items. Discuss the situation with your group and present your recommendations to the class.

V. FOLLOW UP

There are many ways to do business; some are **ethical** and some are not. Do you think the following business practices are ethical or unethical?

1. Giving away free samples to prospective customers

2. Offering to beat any competitor's price

3. False advertising about a product

4. Honoring other store's coupons

5. Bribing government officials

6. Putting out negative publicity about a competitor

7. Lobbying the government to pass laws favorable to your company

8. Industrial espionage (spying on your competitors)

VI. VOCABULARY REVIEW

asset	debt	twist
damage	suspend	analyze
thrive	contention	dramatically
insurance	custodian	thoroughly
contribution	investigate	leaky
utilities	parade	volume
distribute	auditorium	gymnasium
headquarters	bureaucracy	ethical
maintenance	overdue	bribe
competitor	insert	lure
overhead	lottery	sue

TOUCHY SITUATIONS

CHAPTER 13

FOREIGN INVESTMENT

I. WARM UP

Before you begin the activity, consider these questions:

Does the government of your country encourage investment from abroad?

Does it encourage citizens to invest in other countries?

What does your country have to offer other countries?

(natural **resources**, human resources, **capital**, etc.)

What must it **acquire** from other countries?

What are some of the benefits of foreign investment? The disadvantages?

If you had a lot of money, which countries would you invest in?

FOCUS

In this chapter, you will practice business introductions and **negotiation** strategies in English.

II. VOCABULARY PREVIEW/PRONUNCIATION

The following words will appear in this chapter. Your teacher will pronounce them for you.

global	boundary	drawback
proximity	resources	cosmetics
detergent	substantial	enterprise
strike	peripheral	capital
negotiation	stability	component
infrastructure	petroleum	incentive
subsidy	retaliation	barrier
forest	timber	tariff
embargo	literacy	diplomacy
unique	bargain	hesitate

III. CONVERSATION STRATEGIES

BUSINESS INTRODUCTIONS

When introduced by someone else, it is polite to say "How do you do?/It's a pleasure to meet you" to the person you are being introduced to. For example:

> A: Kim, I'd like you to meet Mr. Curtis from Newell-Packer.
> B: How do you do, Mr. Curtis?
> C: It's a pleasure to meet you.

After the introduction, it is common to ask a few questions to get acquainted. For example:

> How long have you been with Safeco?
> Is this your first time to Japan?
> How was your trip (here)?

Sometimes you have to introduce yourself. To do so, use phrases such as:

> I **represent** IVS.
> **I'm with** IVS.
> **We're in the** printing **business.**
> **We sell** electrical components.

(Introductions usually involve a smile, handshake and exchange of business cards.)

ASKING FOR DETAILS

> **What can you tell me about** your country/product?
> **What does your** country **have to offer?**
> **What makes your** country **unique?**

POSITIVE RESPONSE TO INQUIRY

Present your product in a positive but modest manner. Some ideas and phrases are given below:

> We are delighted /honored that you would consider investing in our country.
> You won't be disappointed
> Our people are among the friendliest in the world.
> We are very pleased with the workmanship of our products.
> As you know, we are a small country, but we can offer many **incentives.**

OFFERING INFORMATION/SERVICE

I'll be happy to answer any questions you might have.

Let me know if there is anything I can do for you.

Can I show you a few samples?

NEGOTIATING IN ENGLISH

Business negotiation is a very complex process requiring skill, **diplomacy**, flexibility, and experience. Below are just a few phrases to help you get started.

ASKING FOR SPECIAL DEALS

What incentives can you offer?

What can you offer in terms of tax credits?

What I'd like to know is how the products will be shipped.

EXPRESSING CONCERNS

I'm a little concerned about...

Will there be a problem with...

My major/biggest concern is...

GIVING ASSURANCE

Let me assure you, our products are of the finest quality.

I'm sure we can work something out.

BARGAINING

Would you consider coming down in price?

We are prepared to offer a substantial discount.

We can offer you...

HESITATING/DELAYING

As a sales representative, you may sometimes require time to think over a deal or discuss it with a superior. Some helpful phrases for hesitating or "buying time":

Let me talk it over with my supervisor.

I'll get back to you (on that).

IV. THE SITUATION

Your company has decided to go **global**. For years, all its business has been done within the **boundaries** of Merryland, your home country. With the possibilities of cheaper labor and expanding markets, the board of directors has decided to invest $2 billion overseas. They are most concerned about getting a good return on their investment. The following is a short list of the countries they have chosen as possible investment sites. The final choice will depend on **proximity** to your home country, resources, taxes, government **stability**, etc.

V. YOUR OBJECTIVE

Your teacher will tell you if your are a *business person* hoping to invest in a foreign country, or a *representative of a foreign country* looking for investors.

As a *business person*, your mission is to decide which of the countries is most suitable for your company's investment dollars. If you wish, you may divide your investment budget among several countries. Your teacher will tell you which of the Big 8 companies you represent.

As a *representative of a country*, try to get the companies to invest money and resources in your country. Negotiate a good deal. If you can't find an investor among the Big 8, you may do business with representatives of some of the other countries. Your teacher will tell you which country you represent.

THE BIG 8 (companies)	
Phelix Corporation	computers and peripherals, office machines
Zargon Chemical	chemicals, detergents, soap, cosmetics
Arkatech	telecommunications, electronic components
Steely Motors	automobiles and automobile parts
Pharmacell	food products, drugs
Rendust Petroleum	oil and gasoline, fuel refining
Juno Plastics	small appliances, toys, household goods
KB Electronics	televisions, video, CD and tape players

COUNTRIES TO INVEST IN:

(See details on the following pages.)

Crushia	Verraco	Ollistan	Theragon	Gomania
Oktavia	Fryoland	Spilatia	Plurama	

PROFILE OF PROSPECTIVE INVESTMENT SITES

CRUSHIA
Proximity to Merryland: 3,000 miles
Price of labor: $2 per hour per worker
Quality of work: fair
Business taxes: 6%
Natural resources: timber, oil, coal
Population: 126 million
Literacy: 25%
Major drawbacks: transportation, poverty
Incentives: 2 years tax-free

OLLISTAN
Proximity: 200 miles
Price of labor: $9 per hour
Quality of work: excellent
Business taxes: 22%
Natural resources: water, clean air
Population: 35 million
Literacy: 70%
Major drawbacks: high expenses
Incentives: $1 million tax credit

GOMANIA
Proximity: 6,000 miles away
Price of labor: $7 per hour
Quality of work: good
Business taxes: 10%
Natural resources: oil, gas, good climate
Population: 57 million
Literacy: 60%
Drawbacks: poor record on human rights
Incentives: immediate opening of local market

FRYOLAND
Proximity: 1,500 miles
Price of labor: $6 per hour
Quality of work: very good
Business taxes: 25%
Natural resources: soil, water
Population: 15 million
Literacy: 50%
Major drawbacks: labor strikes
Incentives: discount on shipping

VERRACO
Proximity: 2,000 miles
Price of labor: $3 per hour
Quality of work: good
Business taxes: 8%
Natural resources: coal, iron ore
Population: 65 million
Literacy: 40%
Drawbacks: paying bribes to officials
Incentives: good treatment of foreigners

THERAGON
Proximity: 7,000 miles
Price of labor: $15 per hour
Quality of work: excellent
Business taxes: 40%
Natural resources: gold, copper
Population: 20 million
Literacy: 98%
Drawbacks: restrictions on foreigners
Incentives: quick processing

OKTAVIA
Proximity to Merryland: 1,000 miles
Price of labor: $10 per hour
Quality of work: excellent
Business taxes: 30%
Natural resources: timber, water
Population: 20 million
Literacy: 80% college-educated
Major drawbacks: import tariffs
Incentives: none

SPILATIA
Proximity: 4,000 miles
Price of labor: $8 per hour
Quality of work: good
Business taxes: 12%
Natural resources: natural gas
Population: 80 million
Literacy: 70%
Major drawbacks: lawlessness
Incentives: delayed tax payments

PLURAMA
Proximity: 500 miles away
Price of labor: $5 per hour
Quality of work: very good
Business taxes: 30%
Natural resources: wildlife, forests
Population: 10 million
Literacy: 50%
Major drawbacks: strict tax laws
Incentives: low interest rates

VI. SOMETHING TO THINK ABOUT

In your opinion, are **barriers** to foreign trade good or bad?

What about government subsidies to farmers/agriculture

high-tech industries

other industries

small business

What are your thoughts on the free market/free **enterprise?**

free trade agreements

trading blocs

What types of things do you consider "unfair trading practices"?

What **retaliations** should countries impose against those who practice unfair trade practices?

RELATED ISSUES:

Tariffs	Trade embargoes	Opening markets
Patents	Copyrights	Intellectual property rights

CHAPTER 14

STRANDED IN THE JUNGLE

I. WARM UP

Have you ever been in a situation in which your **survival** depended on someone else?

How dependent or independent are you? Do you work well with others? Think about the statements below and decide which ones are true for you.

I can rely on myself. I am independent.

I need someone to help me achieve my goals.

I can work well with a group.

I can accomplish more when I work alone.

Teamwork produces the best results.

FOCUS

In this chapter you will work as a group to find a way out of a difficult situation. You will learn techniques for outlining and dividing up a complicated task.

II. VOCABULARY/PRONUNCIATION

survival	rescue	stranded
wounded	priority	comrade
hazard	cannibal	terrain
stretcher	raging	cliff
quicksand	guard	panic
pilot	widespread	boil
swamp	drown	responsible
slope	venomous	vegetation
perilous	crash	supper

III. CONVERSATION STRATEGIES

REVIEW OF *IF* STATEMENTS

If Statements were presented in Chapter 11. They can also be used here. For example:

> If we go East, we can cover a greater distance in a short time.
> If we put the wounded on stretchers, we can transport them more easily.

> A: What if it rains?
> B: We can use the plane for shelter.

TALKING ABOUT RISKS

> **Should we take a chance on** crossing the river?
> **What are our chances of** getting out alive?
> **We run the risk of** losing someone.

USING *GET* WITH ADJECTIVES AND PAST PARTICIPLES

Get is sometimes used to indicate what happens *to* a person. In these instances it is followed by an adjective or the past participle of a verb. For example:

> Someone might **get lost.** (adjective)
> **sick** (adjective)
> **hurt** (verb)
> **killed** (verb)
> **bitten** (verb)

EXPRESSING RESERVATIONS

Use modals to express reservations about a particular course of action:

> Splitting up **might be** dangerous.
> Torches **could start** a forest fire.
> That **would cause** widespread panic.

Certain phrases can have the same effect:

> **I don't mean to be** rude, **but** wouldn't that put us at greater risk?
> **I know this sounds** silly, **but** shouldn't we wait till daylight to make a move?

OUTLINING THE TASKS/MAKING ASSIGNMENTS

When a group is working together to solve a problem, it is good to decide what needs to be done and make assignments for doing it. Listed below are various phrases for outlining tasks and making assignments.

DECIDING WHAT SHOULD BE DONE

We need someone to call for help.

cook the food.

go hunting.

stand guard at night.

DIVIDING UP THE TASKS

Who will be responsible for finding shelter?

Who is going to gather firewood?

Who should we put in charge of setting up camp?

Who do you think should take care of the wounded?

ASKING FOR HELP/INPUT

Any volunteers?

Who is willing to come with me?

ASSIGNING

Derrick, **you (can) be responsible for** finding drinking water

Kelvin, **I want you to be in charge of** boiling the water.

Mandy, **would you see if you could** fix the plane?

Laura, you keep the fire going.

AGREEING TO DO A TASK

All right./Sure./No problem.

Whatever you say.

That's fine with me.

It's up to you. (You decide.)

OFFERING YOUR SERVICES

I **could** climb the mountain to survey the area.

Would you like me to keep a lookout for wild animals?

Why don't I fix some supper?

IV. THE SITUATION

You are flying across a dense jungle with the members of your group when your small plane crashes on the top of an inactive volcano. It is 4:30 p.m. The pilot has been killed, three people are injured, and the rest of you are fine. You know that you have landed in an unexplored region of the country and that to survive, you must find your way out.

V. YOUR OBJECTIVE

Discuss each of the options in small groups. Then decide on a proper course of action. After determining what needs to be done, assign members of your group specific tasks to accomplish. You are all in this together, and in order to survive, you must cooperate well.

Your choices, along with their **hazards** and advantages, are listed on the next page.

As you consider the task ahead of you, what do you think your first **priority** should be?

Finding shelter

Finding food

Finding water

Protection from **cannibals**, wild animals, etc.

Taking care of the injured

You and your **comrades** quickly survey the scene. Your options are as follows:

GO NORTH
Terrain: gentle slopes, thick jungle

Hazards: wild animals

Advantages: plenty of food, water

Chances of being rescued: 40%

Chances of getting lost: 60%

GO SOUTH
Terrain: hills, small villages

Hazards: villagers may be cannibals

Advantages: contact with other people

Chances of being rescued: 50%

Chances of being eaten: 50%

GO EAST
Terrain: raging river, cliffs

Hazards: must leave the injured behind

Advantages: food on the other side

Chances of being rescued: 70%

Chances of drowning: 60%

GO WEST
Terrain: open plain, grassland

Hazards: quicksand, swamp

Advantages: not so perilous

Chances of being rescued: 50%

Chances of being seen: 80% by cannibals

70% by airplanes

SPLIT UP
Terrain: varied

Hazards: someone could get killed

Advantages: at least some will survive

Chances of being rescued: 80% (some of you)

Chances of getting lost: 90% (some of you)

STAY PUT
Terrain: mountains, thick vegetation

Hazards: venomous snakes, spiders

Advantages: plane offers protection

Chances of being rescued: 60%

Chances of being bitten: 80%

VI. FOLLOW UP

What is your course of action?

After you have decided on which tasks need to be done and made assignments for the members of your group, prepare to share your plans with the rest of the class.

For example:

We decided that it is best to stay with the plane.

Our reasons for this choice are:

1. _____

2. _____

3. _____

The most important tasks are:

1. _____

2. _____

3. _____

Assignments:

Gary and Deana will go out and look for food.
Troy will take care of the injured.
Marjorie will keep the fire going.

CHAPTER 15

BATTLE OF THE SEXES

I. WARM UP

Men and women have different ways of thinking and feeling. No wonder it is often difficult for them to get along. Below are some common complaints and **stereotypes** which men and women sometimes have about each other. Do you think they are **valid**? Have you ever used them in talking about the opposite sex?

Common complaints by women about men.

> He never listens to me.
> He doesn't say "I love you" enough.
> He is only interested in sex.
> He's always looking at other women.
> He doesn't spend enough time with me and the kids.

Common complaints by men about women.

> She's too emotional.
> She talks too much.
> She can't make up her mind.
> She doesn't pay enough attention to my needs.
> She is always **nagging** me.

Common stereotypes:

> Men are logical; women are emotional.
> Men use love to get sex. Women use sex to get love.
> Men are concerned with **tangible** things. (cars, electronic equipment, etc.)
> Women are concerned with relationships.

Focus

In this chapter, you will have an opportunity to explore and discuss the problems that sometimes arise between the sexes. Keep an open mind. You might learn something new.

II. CONVERSATION STRATEGIES

In your discussions for this chapter, you will likely encounter some ideas that you may not have thought of before. People have various reactions to new ideas. Some phrases for expressing the different reactions are given below.

ACKNOWLEDGEMENT

Hmmm.
I didn't know that.
I didn't realize that.
Is that true?

EXPRESSING DISBELIEF

There are several ways to express disbelief in a new idea. One way is with simple questions:

Do you really agree with that?
Do you really think so?
Why do you say that?
What makes you say that?
Are you serious?

Another way is by questioning a person's meaning

Do you mean to say that women are more energetic than men?
Do you mean to tell me that I don't understand a man's point of view?
Are you saying that women have it easier than men?
Are you suggesting that child care is more important than making a living?

An even more emphatic way to express disbelief is to restate a person's idea with rising intonation as if asking a question. For example:

Men are more frugal than women?
Women have stronger bodies than men?
You mean that *I* don't understand women?
You mean to say that men shouldn't watch sports on TV?

For added effect, say each word slowly and clearly or pause shortly after words or phrases that you wish to emphasize. For example:

Are you trying to tell me—that men—are more reasonable—than women?
I can't believe—that you think—*I'm*—insensitive.

Negative statements can also be used to express disbelief:

> You **don't mean that** women can handle their emotions better than men.
>
> You're **not suggesting that** I'm insecure.
>
> **Don't tell me that** you believe it too.

Other expressions to emphatically express disbelief or shock are:

> **What in the world** are you talking about?
>
> **What on earth** do you mean?
>
> **How can you say that?**
>
> **I can't believe** you'd say that.
>
> You **must be kidding.**
>
> You **can't be serious.**
>
> **Are you crazy?**
>
> **No way!**

CLARIFYING/PARAPHRASING

One of the best ways to clarify your own idea is to rephrase it. Noun clauses are very useful for this.

> **Example:**
>
> **What I mean is** that's very inconsiderate.
>
> **What I'm trying to say is…**
>
> **What I would do is…**
>
> **What happened is…**

Noun clauses can also be used to paraphrase another's idea:

> **What you're trying to say is…**
>
> **What he means is…**

Other common phrases are

> **By that, I mean…**
>
> **He really means that…**

III. THE SITUATIONS

The following are situations in which misunderstanding, sometimes even conflict, may occur between men and women. Discuss the situations with your partner (preferably someone of the opposite sex) and decide what these couples should do. This is not a role play.

1. John consistently comes home late from work without telling his wife, Mary, the reason. Mary thinks that he should at least phone her and let her know where he is. What do you think?

2. Mrs. Nagg is constantly **griping** about her husband's lack of **ambition** in his job. She feels that by now he should be vice-president of his company. She also complains that he doesn't do his share of the housework. What is your opinion of this situation?

3. Mr. Stonewall never talks to his wife anymore. As soon as he gets home from work, he plops down in front of the TV and expects Mrs. Stonewall to **cater** to him like a maid. What is your opinion of this situation?

4. Arnold is a **slob**. He never cleans up after himself and doesn't mind if the house looks like a pig pen. Betty, on the other hand, is a **perfectionist**. She expects her home to be **spotless** 24 hours a day. How can they resolve this problem?

5. Russell and Erica have been married for less than a year and already Erica is looking around at other men. Russell thinks his wife should get a job rather than staying home and watching **soap operas** all day. Erica's mother-in-law thinks they should have a baby. What do you think?

6. Cassie suspects her husband, Norman, is **having an affair**. Last night he came home with **lipstick** on his **collar**. Norman denies any wrongdoing. Should Cassie press the issue and risk losing her husband? They have three small children.

7. Shortly after their **honeymoon**, Douglas and Erma realized how **incompatible** they were. They are totally opposite in personality, attitudes toward money and approaches to doing things. They don't have a single hobby in common. Do you think this marriage will survive?

8. Alice has a terrible **snoring** habit. Her husband, Philip, can't stand the noise and ends up sleeping on the couch with a pillow over his head. What should they do?

9. Al and Sue are getting a **divorce**. Sue says that Al hit her once and gave her a black eye. Al says she deserved it. Is there anything they can do to save this marriage?

10. Louise expected Gerald to be like her father, bringing her flowers, remembering birthdays and **anniversaries** and constantly **reaffirming** his love for her. Gerald thinks his wife is being unrealistic. Should he change to fit her image of a perfect husband?

11. Mr. Boring complains that since they had their first child, his wife does nothing to keep herself attractive. He remembers that as a **newlywed**, Mrs. Boring was the most beautiful woman on earth. Is he being unreasonable to expect his wife to remain attractive after having children?

12. Lucille complains that Floyd never helps with the baby. For example, he never changes **diapers**, mixes milk formula or holds the baby when she is crying. He says that since he works eight hours a day to provide for his family, he deserves a little rest when he gets home. What is your opinion?

13. Mr. and Mrs. Bradley have two children. Mr. Bradley is very strict and thinks that children should be punished for every mistake. His wife, on the other hand, is quite lenient and feels that children will discover what is right and wrong from their own experience. The Bradleys are always arguing about discipline. How can they solve this problem?

14. Oliver and Flora have been married for 25 years. Flora's only complaint is that her husband likes to look at other women, especially young beautiful ones. Oliver says that he would never leave his wife but he still "appreciates works of art" when he sees them. Do you think Flora has a valid concern or that she should lighten up?

IV. FOR FURTHER DISCUSSION

Think about the following questions and be prepared to share your opinions with the class.

In your opinion, is it more important to love or to be loved?

If you had to choose between (A) someone you loved (but he/she didn't love you) and (B) someone who loved you (but you didn't love him/her), which would you choose?

AGREE OR DISAGREE?

If a man truly loves his wife, he will never look at or **flirt** with another woman.

If you are an attractive woman, it is okay for other women's husbands to admire you.

If your spouse is attractive, it is okay for people of the opposite sex to admire him/her.

V. VOCABULARY REVIEW

stereotype	attract(ive)	flirt
newlywed	honeymoon	cater
slob	spotless	soap opera
(in)compatible	gripe	reaffirm
lighten up	snore	diaper
valid	anniversary	perfectionist
lipstick	collar	have an affair
frugal	divorce	logical
ambition	tangible	nag

CHAPTER 16

BUDGET CUTS

I. WARM UP

PRELIMINARY QUESTIONS

As a taxpayer, how do you think the **funds** for a government–run university should be spent?

Would your opinions differ if you were the university president? a student?

What should the main goal of a public university be?

> education of its students
> education of the community
> non–profit **research** projects
> **profit** making research projects
> providing entertainment and **recreation facilities** to the public
> sponsoring **forums** and **seminars** for the academic community
> other

Do you think a university should try to **break even** financially?

Of all the methods for financing a university, which do you most agree with?

> raising **tuition**
> investing university **assets**
> profit–making **schemes**
> asking **alumni** for funds
> seeking research **grants** from large corporations
> accepting **donations** from private organizations or individuals

FOCUS

In this chapter, you will practice discussion skills and learn how to make proposals. Before you begin, you may wish to review presentation strategies from chapters 4 and 8.

II. CONVERSATION STRATEGIES

NUMBERING/LISTING

The most common way to list ideas is to use ordinal numbers (first, second, third, etc.) Another way is to say the numbers themselves. For example:

We could eliminate the budget deficit by **1)** reducing all travel expenditures, **2)** spending less on research, and **3)** raising tuition. (Say *one*, *two*, and *three*.)

INTERRUPTING

Some phrases for interrupting during a discussion are listed below:

Excuse me for interrupting, but...

May I interrupt?

Let me interject something here.

Do you mind if I break in here?

Can I say something here?

interrupt

jump in

NOTE: While you may interrupt informal discussions using the phrases above or something similar, it is not polite to interrupt another person when there are only two of you talking. Also, do not interrupt formal speeches. Sometimes a lecturer may give you permission to interrupt his presentation with questions or comments, but it is courteous to raise your hand and wait for him/her to call on you.

CONJECTURING

Sometimes you may be called on to make an intelligent guess or estimation of time, costs, etc. Some phrases for this are:

I **estimate that** it would cost $3 million.

It **would probably** take a few thousand dollars.

My **guess is that** it would take 5 months.

ADDING A COMMENT

If you would like to contribute additional ideas, you can use phrases such as

Not only that but...

I might add that...

In addition to that...

It wouldn't hurt to mention that...

PRESENTATION SKILLS

MAKING A PROPOSAL

Formal presentations before high level administrators (CEOs, boards of directors, school officials, etc.) often involve making proposals. Good proposals will show your superiors that you have thought carefully about the implications and effects of what you are proposing.

Proposals often include these elements:

Statement of proposed course of action

Reasons for action/change

Lists of benefits to company/university/organization

Costs to company/organization

Plans for implementation

Timetable

In this chapter, you will have practice making simple proposals. A sample outline is given below:

Main statement:	Our committee would like to propose that the university continue the following programs: _____, _____ and _____.
Benefits:	The _____ would benefit the university in a number of ways: _____, _____ and _____.
Costs:	The project will cost us... We intend to fund this by...
Concluding Remarks:	We appreciate your careful consideration of our proposal.

III. THE SITUATION

The university president just announced that the government, which sponsors your institution, is cutting your budget by fifteen million dollars. This means that some of the programs you had planned will have to be taken off the agenda. The following proposals were slated for this fiscal year. Now only seven of them can be approved. Your finance committee must decide which programs to cut and which to keep.

IV. YOUR OBJECTIVE

As a group, decide which of the following projects you will leave on the budget and which ones you will **eliminate** (you may **retain** only 7). Then make a proposal based on your decisions and be prepared to present it to the class.

New football **stadium**

Natural sciences **museum**

Annex to the university library

Funding for cancer research

Research on supercomputers

Medical school equipment (needs to be **upgraded**)

MBA program (scheduled to open in three years)

Wildlife preserve

Scholarships for low-income students

New **dormitories** for students

Fine arts hall

University bookstore expansion

Education Week for the local community

Shelter for the homeless

V. SOMETHING TO THINK ABOUT

Do you think university (or government) officials deserve all their perks (perquisites)?

Which of the following do you think they deserve, and which ones should be eliminated?

free housing

company car and **chauffeur**

family insurance plan

tax–free income

free access to all university facilities/events

paid vacations

paid travel anywhere in the world

freedom from **prosecution** (for diplomats and government officials)

large office staff

free education for spouse and children

equivalent benefits extended to entire family

moving expenses

Do you think religious or **moral** instruction has a place in public education? If so, who should sponsor it?

VI. VOCABULARY REVIEW

recreation	scholarship	prosecution
research	stadium	equivalent
forum	museum	conjecture
seminar	upgrade	implementation
tuition	interject	dormitory
scheme	eliminate	profit
donation	chauffeur	annex
slated	fiscal	remark
retain	perk	implication
fund	moral	alumni

CHAPTER 17

YOUR DREAM HOME

I. WARM UP

What types of homes do most people in your country live in?

Single dwelling
Farm house
Suburban home
Mansion
Hut

Multiple dwelling
Apartments
Government housing
Condominiums
Duplex

Do couples in your country continue to live with their parents after marriage?

Do young people typically move out when they go to college? Why or why not?

Can young couples in your country afford to buy their own homes?

Do many families in your country save up to build their own homes?

What are the obstacles to buying a home?

How do couples finance their homes? Do they borrow money from parents, relatives, a bank or loan agency?

FOCUS

In this chapter, you will practice sales vocabulary and phrases as you go shopping for household items.

Vocabulary will be presented at the end of the chapter.

II. CONVERSATION STRATEGIES

SHOPPING

Review the shopping vocabulary and expressions from Chapter 9. Some additional phrases are listed below:

I'm looking for a vacuum cleaner.

I need to get a new mattress.

Do you have any irons?

Sample conversation:

A: Can I help you find something?

B: Yes, do you have any **blenders**?

A: We sure do. They're on the second **shelf** next to the toasters.

SELLING POINTS

As a salesperson, you want to make your customer aware of the special features of your product. Some helpful phrases for listing selling points of a product are given below.

This brand features a standard keyboard.

This model has a built-in freezer and ice maker.

(Refer to Chapter 8 for more phrases explaining the features of a product.)

DISCUSSING PRODUCTS

When buying "big-ticket" (highly priced) items, it is important to discuss many things with the salesperson:

Price

Warranties

Delivery

Terms of Payment

As a salesperson, you may use the above factors to offer the customer a better deal. If a customer starts to walk away without buying anything, you might say:

I can give you a special price on this one.

This item has a five-year warranty

We can deliver it for you.

Can I show you a less expensive model?

It comes in different sizes.

DECLINING A SALESPERSON'S HELP

If, as a customer, you are reluctant to accept a salesperson's offer or have reservations about purchasing a product, you might say:

(No,) **I'm just looking** today.

I'm just browsing.

I think **I'll look around a little more.**

Thanks for your help. We'll (go home and) **think about it.**

FURTHER BUSINESS

In order to get more business, a salesperson might ask:

Will there be anything else?

Is that all for today?

Can I get you anything else?

DISCUSSING TERMS OF PAYMENT

Some big items (appliances, furniture) require that the customers make a deposit or "put some money down" before he can take the item with them. Some phrases for this are:

It requires a **down payment** of $50.

(There's) **no money down.**

A salesperson might offer the customer flexible terms of payment if a customer seems concerned about money.

Will that be cash or credit?

You may **pay in installments.**

Would you like me to put that on your **account**?

We have a **30-day return policy.**

III. THE SITUATION

You and your spouse have been saving up all of your married life for a new home. Now the time has finally arrived for you to move out of the small apartment you have been renting and into the dream home that you have just built. You have some extra money for new furnishings and **fixtures** but must spend it carefully and only on those items you think are essential for your new home.

IV. YOUR OBJECTIVE

Today you will go on a shopping spree for things to put in your new house.

This is a partner <u>and</u> group activity. There are four steps:

1. PARTNER DISCUSSION

Look over the lists on the next page and discuss with your partner (spouse) the things you really need/want for your new home. You can afford three items from each category.

2. DIVISION OF TASKS

You and your spouse own one of the 8 shops listed on the next page. (Your teacher may give you a card indicating which one.) One of you must mind the store while the other goes shopping. In other words, one partner stays where she is and plays the role of a shopkeeper receiving customers from among her classmates. The other partner is a customer, who must walk around to the various "stores," which are selling household goods. You decide which partner will do what.

3. BUYING/SELLING:

As a **salesperson,** your objective is to get the others to buy as much as possible in your shop.

As a **customer,** you need to save your money and get the best deals.

4. FOLLOW UP:

After you have finished shopping, return to your partner and tell him/her what you bought for your new home.

LIST OF HOUSEHOLD PRODUCTS SHOPS

Reliable Appliances, Inc.	Pipeline Bathroom Fixtures
Refrigerator	Bathtub
Washer	Shower
Dryer	Toilet
Dishwasher	Wash basin (bathroom sink)
Dish dryer	Hot tub
Microwave oven	Shower curtain
Range (stove)	Medicine cabinet

Comfy Home Furnishings	Sleepy Z Bedroom Supply
Sofa (couch)	King–size bed
Armchair(s)	Bunk beds
Home entertainment center	Night stands
Coffee table	Dresser
Area rug	Chest of **drawers**
Bookcase	Mirrors
Lazy chair (recliner)	Crib

Moonbeam Electrical Supply	Kitchen Outlet
Chandeliers	Toaster
Table lamps	Electric mixer
Fancy lights	Automatic rice cooker
Iron and ironing board	Blender
Vacuum cleaner	Dining room set
Home computer	Electric frying pan
Garbage **disposal**	Coffee maker

Bracken Becker Outdoor Supply	Miscellaneous (To be supplied by building contractor.)
Gardening tools	Fireplace
Lawn mower	Two–car garage and **driveway**
Wheelbarrow	Unfinished basement
Sprinkler system	**Patio**
Barbeque set	Cupboards
Wooden **fence**	Kitchen **cabinets**
Storage **shed**	Closets

V. SOMETHING TO THINK ABOUT

Discuss these questions as a class:

1. How many of the items on the previous page can you live without? Which ones do you think are necessities?.

2. What are the minimum requirements of a good home (for a family of four)?
   utilities (water, gas, electricity, telephone)
   rooms (which kind and how many of each?)
   furniture and fixtures

3. How do you feel about buying things on credit?

4. Do you understand the term "mortgage?" Do you think its a good idea?

5. What type of neighborhood do you prefer to live in?
   Rural, Suburban, Urban

VI. VOCABULARY REVIEW

dwelling	condominium	obstacle
suburban	duplex	furniture
fixture	chandelier	vacuum cleaner
iron	blender	drawer
fence	barbecue	wheelbarrow
sprinkler	fireplace	lawn mower
patio	cupboard	cabinet
closet	appliance	shed
mattress	mortgage	toaster
shelf	reluctant	down payment
policy	browse	disposal

CHAPTER 18

POLITICAL REFUGEES

Indicate whether you agree or disagree with the following statements:

1. All **citizens** should obey the laws of their countries.

2. No laws are unjust.

3. Governments should guarantee freedom and basic human rights to all citizens.

4. Governments have an obligation to protect their citizens.

5. Governments have a right to control people's actions.

6. If people don't like the country they are living in, they should be free to leave.

7. It is okay to break the law if your motives are pure.

8. Governments should allow individuals who are seeking political asylum into their countries without restriction.

9. If people enter a country illegally, they should be deported to the country of origin.

FOCUS

In this chapter, you will have a chance to review the discussion skills you have learned thus far. Since it is a review, no new conversation strategies will be given.

Vocabulary is presented at the end of the chapter.

II. THE SITUATION

Freedonia is a wealthy but crowded nation. Its people enjoy a high standard of living and a democratic system of government. They are free to travel anywhere and any time they want.

Desparta is a very poor country and its people suffer not only from poverty but also from a totalitarian government which greatly restricts their freedoms. Because of their hardships, many of Desparta's people want to immigrate to Freedonia. However, their government doesn't allow any unauthorized travel, and any person who is caught trying to escape will be tortured or maybe even killed.

The border between the two countries is a 3 km wide river which is infested with hungry sharks. There is only one bridge between the countries, and it is patrolled by guards and vicious dogs.

Freedonia will accept some, but not all, political refugees who successfully cross the border into their country from Desparta.

III. YOUR OBJECTIVE

You are a part of a government **panel** in Freedonia. Your job is to review each refugee's case and decide who may stay and who must go back to Desparta. You may accept all, none, or some of the refugees. Which of the following will you allow to stay and which will you send back? Discuss each case with the members of your group and mark "S" for "stay" and "D" for "deport".

1. A man successfully swims across the river to Freedonia.

   _____

2. A man steals a boat and takes it across the river to Freedonia.

   _____

3. A young boy runs across the bridge. He is chased by border dogs and bitten badly. Eventually, he makes it to Freedonia but must be put in the hospital.

   _____

4. A young girl races her motorcycle across the bridge and breaks the border gate. She crashes on Freedonia's side of the border. She is seriously injured but not killed.

   _____

5. A man assaults a fisherman at night. Then he and his family use the fisherman's boat to cross the river. The fisherman is knocked **unconscious** but is not killed.

   _____

6. A man and his family construct a hot air balloon and ride it to Freedonia.

   _____

7. A woman acquires a **phony** passport. After she enters the country illegally, she is **apprehended** by the Freedonia police and put into jail. She **pleads** for freedom.

   _____

8. An air force pilot from Desparta and his co-pilot fly their aircraft across the border and land it in Freedonia's military airport. Both seek asylum in Desparta.

   _____

9. A man bribes the border guards with $10,000 and they allow him to pass through the gate.

   _____

10. A beautiful young woman sleeps with a border guard, and he allows her through the border gate the next day.

    _____

11. A young man obtains permission and a passport from Desparta's government. After he arrives in Freedonia legally, he refuses to return.

_____

12. A woman **hijacks** a plane and forces it to land in Freedonia's main airport. No one is harmed in the incident.

_____

13. A young couple put their two year old son into a metal box and he **floats** across the river to Freedonia. The boy is found by a family who want to adopt him.

_____

14. A young woman from Desparta has a boyfriend in Freedonia. One night, the boy rents a motorized watercraft and crosses the river to pick her up. They both travel back to Freedonia safely.

_____

15. A man robs a bank in Desparta and uses the money to buy a boat which he takes to Freedonia.

_____

16. An old man hides in a meat truck **heading** to Freedonia from Desparta. After he successfully crosses the border without being caught, he walks out to freedom.

_____

17. An Olympic **athlete** attends a **tournament** in Freedonia. After practice one night she **sneaks** out of the dormitory and asks to become a citizen of Freedonia.

_____

18. A man tries to run across the border but is seen by one of the guards. When the guard starts to chase him, the man takes out a gun and shoots the guard. Then he successfully gets across the bridge to Freedonia.

_____

19. A border guard who is tired of his job and life in Desparta walks across the bridge and asks the officials of Freedonia to let him in.

_____

20. A teenage girl runs away from home in Desparta and somehow **makes it** to Freedonia. Her parents demand that she be returned to them.

_____

IV. SOMETHING TO THINK ABOUT

After you have made your decisions, consider the following questions. Be prepared to share your answers in a class discussion.

1. Would it make any difference if any of these people were **economic** rather than political refugees?

2. Did you make your decisions on a case-by-case basis, or did you have some **underlying** principle which governed your decisions?

   Examples of underlying principles:

   > Everyone who wants freedom is **entitled** to have it **regardless** of the means they use to obtain it.

   > If a person commits a crime, he should be punished regardless of the individual circumstances surrounding his crime.

3. Did any of the following things affect your decisions?

   The age of the refugee

   The sex of the refugee

   Whether or not a crime had been committed

   The seriousness of the crime

   The bravery of the person's escape from Desparta

   Whether or not the person was healthy

   The usefulness of the individual to Freedonia

V. VOCABULARY REVIEW

The following words appear in Chapter 18. Write down what you think each one means.

poverty	athlete	totalitarian
panel	immigrate	citizen
torture	economic	vicious
sneak	infest	entitle
(be infested with)	(be entitled to)	shark
underlying	patrol	tournament
hardship	unjust	unauthorized
float	restrict	regardless (of)
refugee	hijack	unconscious
plead	guarantee	apprehend
asylum	obligation	phony
deport	heading	make it

After you have guessed the meanings of the above words, check with your teacher or the dictionary to see how many you got correct.

CHAPTER 19

WISHFUL THINKING

I. WARM UP

In Chapter 11, you learned how to use **if statements** to talk about present decisions and future consequences. In this chapter, you will learn a different kind of **if statement**, which deals with things that are only imagined or wished for.

Compare the following:

If I **have** some money left over, I **will buy** a horse.

(possibly in the future)

present tense   *future tense (same as those in Chapter 11)*

If I **had** some money, I **would buy** a horse.

(I don't have money now)

past tense   *would + verb*

If I **had had** some money, I **would have bought** a horse.

(I didn't have money then)

past perfect tense   *would + have + past participle*

FOCUS

The above statements talk about situations, not as they really are, but as the speaker wishes or imagines them to be. This chapter will explain these types of statements in more detail and let you practice them in conversational contexts.

II. VOCABULARY PREVIEW/PRONUNCIATION

stuck	commute	wages
battery	pearl	necklace
cashier	ring up	expressway
wax	worth	show up
landlord	evict	rural
charity	stage	alarm
raffle	postage	daydream
predicament	puddle	curb
splash	tuxedo	gown

III. CONVERSATION STRATEGIES

Sometimes people cannot change their current condition, but wish they could. They might wonder or daydream about what it would be like if they were in a different situation. In such cases, a special type of **if statement** is used to express their desires.

For example:

1. Real Situation: I don't have a sports car.
2. Present Wish: I wish I **had** a sports car.
3. *Imagined* Situation: *If* I **had** a sports car, I **would be** popular.

Notice that even though this is a *present* situation, the **past tense** is used in both 2 and 3 to indicate that the ideas are only imagined.

IV. YOUR OBJECTIVE

With a partner, make conversations using **if statements** to talk about imagined situations.

SAMPLE SITUATION

You want to buy a sailboat, but because you live in Wyoming, which is far away from the ocean, you cannot use one. You want to move to California where you can easily buy and enjoy a fancy sailboat.

Example:

A: Why are you so unhappy?

B: I wish I **lived** in California

A: Why is that?

B: Because if I **lived** in California, I **would own** a sailboat.

A: California? You really want to go there?

B: Doesn't everybody?

A: Not me. I wish I **lived** in Hawaii.

V. SOME SITUATIONS

1. You work for Forbes Motor Company but would rather work for Crystal. Crystal Motors pays higher wages.

   _____

2. You are married but would rather be single. You think single people have more fun.

   _____

3. Your friends went to the beach today. You wish you could be with them, but you had to come to work.

   _____

4. You are locked in the basement. You wish you had a hammer to help you get out. Call your partner on the telephone and explain your predicament.

   _____

5. You spend a lot of money on cigarettes. Your partner thinks you should give up the habit. (Try "If you didn't smoke…")

   _____

6. Shelly doesn't think Shawn loves her because he won't buy her a pearl necklace. What might she say to him? (Hint: "If you really loved me…")

   _____

7. You must commute 20 miles to your university classes every day. You would rather live in the dormitories on campus so you could save travel time.

   _____

NOTE: The verb **were** is used in *present* wishes and **if statements** requiring a "be" verb regardless of the subject. For example:

> I wish I **were** a doctor.
> If I **were** a doctor, I would be rich
> He wishes he **were** not here.
> If he **were** not here, he would be home in bed.

LOOKING BACK WITH IF STATEMENTS

The second type of **if statement** presented in this chapter is a little more complicated.

To talk about past decisions/actions that you wish had been different, use past perfect tense in the **if clause**. The verbs in the main statement or clause will depend on whether you are referring to the present or the past:

Examples:

I wish I **hadn't drunk** so much last night. Now I **feel** terrible.
If I **hadn't drunk** so much last night, I **wouldn't feel** so terrible.
      (past action)   (present consequence)

I wish I **hadn't drunk** so much last night. I **felt** terrible **then**.
If I **hadn't drunk** so much last night, I **wouldn't have felt** so terrible.
      (past action)   (past consequence)

I wish I **had left** home sooner. I **was** late for the party last night.
If I **had left** home earlier, I **wouldn't have been** late for the party.
      (past action)   (past consequence)

I wish I **had left** home sooner. Now I **am** stuck in traffic.
If I **had left** home sooner, I **wouldn't be** stuck in traffic.
      (past action)   (present consequence)

With a partner, practice past wishes and **if statements** in the following situations:

1. You didn't study computer science in college. Now your boss will not give you a promotion because you cannot operate a computer.

   _____

2. Your partner parked in a No-parking zone for five minutes yesterday. He/She got a parking ticket.

   _____

3. You forgot to send out Christmas cards last year. Several of your friends refuse to talk with you now.

   _____

4. It is your daughter's wedding day. You forgot to order a wedding cake. Now all the bakeries in town are closed.

   _____

5. You missed the final basket worth two points. Your basketball team lost the game by only one point. You feel awful.

_____

6. The plane you were supposed to be on just took off for Cincinnati. Your taxi driver didn't take the **expressway,** and you had to spend an extra hour in traffic.

_____

7. You left your term paper, which was due today, on the coffee table. The dog ate it. Now you think you will fail the course.

_____

8. You stood too close to the **curb.** A speeding car drove through a mud **puddle** and **splashed** water all over your **tuxedo**/evening **gown.**

_____

MORE CONVERSATION STRATEGIES

In the above situations, the focus was on using the **if statements** themselves. These types of statements are seldom used outside of a larger conversation. To make the interaction more natural and authentic, a conversational context is needed. Below are some phrases to help you incorporate **if statements** into conversation.

STARTING A CONVERSATION

When you can tell someone has been having a difficult time, you can open a conversation with:

What seems to be the problem?

Is everything all right?

Can I help you with something?

For example:

A: Is everything all right?

B: Not really. You see, my car broke down and I had to walk to work this morning. I was 25 minutes late.

A: Why didn't you call me? **If I had known, I would have given** you a ride.

GIVING RETROSPECTIVE ADVICE

Modals (*should, could, might, must, may, would*) can be used with **have** and the **past participle** to show how something may have happened differently. They can also be used to give retrospective advice (tell how a situation could have been handled better).

A: I didn't win anything in the raffle.
B: You **should have bought** more tickets. I **would have sold** you some.

A: Did you get the part?
B: No, I really blew it.
A: What happened?
B: I tripped on stage.
A: You **should have been** more careful.

A: I didn't hear my alarm this morning
B: You **must have forgotten** to set it.

A: You know what?
B: What?
A: My letter was sent back to me by the post office.
B: You **must not have put** enough postage on it.

A: I threw away a lot of food after the party last night.
B: You **could've given** it to me.
Or: You **could have donated** it to charity.

Another way to give retrospective advice is to use questions like, **Why did you... ?** or **Why didn't you... ?** For example:

A: I missed the bus last night and had to take a taxi.
B: **Why didn't you call me?** I **would have come** to pick you up.

A: My car battery is dead.
B: **Why did you** leave the lights on?
Or: **Why didn't you** turn the lights off?

NOTE: Students often mix up the word order in these types of questions. Be careful.

Why you didn't answer the phone last night?   Incorrect
Why didn't you answer the phone last night?   Correct

VI. PUTTING IT ALL TOGETHER

The following situations give you a chance to review **if statements** and to practice giving retrospective advice. Work with a partner to create conversations which incorporate what you have learned.

1. You didn't learn to type in high school. Now you must pay Miss Steno a fortune to type your papers for you. Discuss the situation with your partner.

   _____

2. Your partner went to the dentist today. She had six cavities. She knows she shouldn't have eaten so much candy during the holidays.

   _____

3. You didn't pay your rent on time. Now your **landlord** is going to **evict** you. Ask your partner to lend you some money.

   _____

4. You finished your term paper yesterday, but may have left it at the copy center or the coffee shop. Discuss with your partner where you think it might be.

   _____

5. You went skiing and broke your leg. Now you can't go ice skating on Saturday.

   _____

6. You didn't wash the dishes or wax the floor yesterday. Aunt Vera **showed up** unexpectedly and you were embarrassed about your house. Tell you partner about it.

   _____

7. You went to the supermarket to buy some groceries. After the **cashier** had **rung up** your sale of $104.59, you realized that you had left your purse/wallet on the kitchen table with all your money, credit cards, and checkbook in it. Phone your partner and tell him/her about your problem.

   _____

8. As you sit down to take the final exam, your professor announces that the test will be "open book". You left your book and notes at home.

   _____

CHAPTER 20

PRESENT YOUR CASE

I. WARM UP

Do you believe that some people are more likely to commit a crime than others? If so, what kind of people?

What are the major factors determining whether a person will commit a crime or not?

- chances of getting away with it (not getting caught)
- availability of "tools" needed to commit the crime
- revenge against another person
- sufficient motive
- curiosity
- greed/strong desire for something
- mental instability
- nature of the person

FOCUS

In this chapter, you will have a chance to review the conversation strategies you have learned as you determine whether an accused person is innocent or guilty.

II. VOCABULARY PREVIEW/PRONUNCIATION

obvious	evidence	stab
fingerprint	butcher	glove
outraged	butler	jealous
innocent	guilty	revenge
penalty	motive	curiosity
jury	accuse	alibi
struggle	will (noun)	estate
inconsiderate	workaholic	plumber
meticulous	impulsive	disguised
petition	grudge	inherit

III. CONVERSATION STRATEGIES

STATING THE FACTS

The facts are...

The fact is...

It is clear that...

It is obvious that...

The evidence points to...

EMPHASIZING A POINT

I would like to point out that...

I would like to bring to your attention the fact that...

I would like to submit that...

EXPRESSING DOUBTS

I doubt that...

I wouldn't bet on it.

MAKING ASSERTIONS

I'll bet that...

I wouldn't be surprised if...

I have a hunch that...

ADDING NEW PERSPECTIVES

That brings up/raises the issue of...

That presents the problem of...

PRESENTING YOUR CASE

I will attempt to show that...

We will prove that...

The evidence will show that...

PRESENTATION STRATEGIES

Below is a sample outline, which can help you make your presentation:

We will show that on____(date)____, ____(name of suspect)____ brutally murdered Major Mint in his penthouse apartment.

The facts of the case are clear:

1. _____

2. _____

3. _____

4. _____

5. _____

Therefore, ____(name of suspect)____ is without a doubt guilty of first degree murder.

IV. THE SITUATION

Major Mint was found dead in his penthouse apartment last night at 10:30 p.m. He had been **stabbed** three times in the heart with a **butcher** knife. He was found lying face-up on his bed, and there was no sign of a **struggle**. A pair of diamond **earrings** are missing from his wife's jewelry box. No **fingerprints** were found on the body or weapon, as the murderer was wearing gloves. The front door was unlocked and the watchdog was sound asleep.

Just last week Mr. Mint made out a **will** leaving most of his **estate** to his younger brother, Spiro. His older brother, Brett, was **outraged**. Most of the major's friends have abandoned him because of his shady business practices. It is also widely known that he was having an affair with his secretary and that his wife was thinking of filing for divorce.

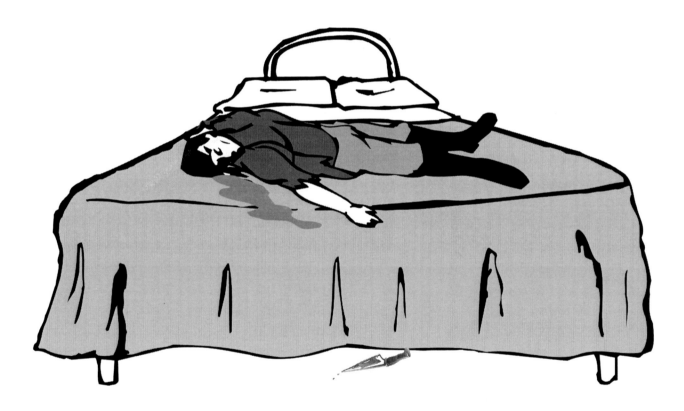

V. YOUR OBJECTIVE

Each of the following suspects has been **accused** of murdering Major Mint. Discuss each one with your group and decide who did it. Then present your findings to the class. Also, be prepared to state why you think the others are innocent.

SUSPECT #1

Name: Spiro Mint

Relationship to Major Mint: younger brother

Motive: getting the money before his brother changed his mind

Alibi: says he was attending a "charity ball" with his wife

Positive (character) traits: very generous

Negative traits: lazy, unemployed

Unanswered question: Where did you get the money for that beautiful new house?

SUSPECT #2

Name: Tempra Mint

Relationship to Major Mint: wife

Motive: is the main beneficiary in husband's life insurance policy

Alibi: says she was having dinner with a "friend"

Positive traits: ambitious and practical

Negative traits: extremely jealous

Unanswered question: How much money would you get if your husband died *after* the divorce?

SUSPECT #3

Name: Brett Mint

Relationship to Major Mint: older brother

Motive: was angry that Spiro would inherit so much of the major's estate

Alibi: says he was at the office, of course

Positive traits: hard working

Negative traits: rude and inconsiderate

Unanswered question: Why haven't you spoken to the major for over two years?

SUSPECT #4

Name: Ruby Dovey

Relationship to Major Mint: secretary

Motive: was upset because the major never bought her any jewelry

Alibi: says she was playing tennis with her "nephew"

Positive traits: kindhearted

Negative traits: selfish, absent–minded

Unanswered question: When did you start wearing that expensive diamond ring?

SUSPECT #5

Name: Howard Aino

Relationship to Major Mint: butler

Motive: was secretly in love with the major's wife

Alibi: went out to "run some errands"

Positive traits: very loyal to the Mints

Negative traits: cannot control his emotions

Unanswered question: Why did Mr. Mint recently threaten to fire you?

SUSPECT #6

Name: Wanda Rays

Relationship to Major Mint: maid

Motive: was unhappy because she didn't get the salary increase she asked for

Alibi: went out to "buy some spices" for Mr. Mint's dinner

Positive traits: meticulous, well-organized

Negative traits: holds grudges for a long time

Unanswered question: Why did you recently sharpen all the knives in the house?

SUSPECT #7

Name: Arty Swindle

Relationship to Major Mint: former business partner

Motive: the major recently cheated him out of $5 million

Alibi: says he was at the bank depositing a check

Positive traits: very smart

Negative traits: sneaky, dishonest

Unanswered question: What information did Mr. Mint give to the FBI about you?

SUSPECT #8

Name: B. D. Ives

Relationship to Major Mint: none whatsoever

Motive: a well-known jewelry thief

Alibi: says he was "jogging in the park"

Positive traits: provides well for his family

Negative traits: impulsive

Unanswered question: Why did you visit the major's house last week disguised as a plumber?

VI. FOLLOW UP

Consider the following questions:

If you were on a jury, how would you determine whether a person was **guilty** or **innocent**?

In this activity, you were asked to find one suspect guilty. What are some other possible solutions?

Conspiracy?

Frame–Up?

Suicide?

Self–defense?

If you could have one more clue to solve the mystery, what would it be?

If you were a detective questioning each of the suspects, what would you ask them?

What is the difference between first–degree (premeditated) and second–degree murder?

What do you think the penalty for first degree murder should be?

Death

Life imprisonment

Other